PROJECTIONS
of the
CONSCIOUSNESS
A Diary of Out-Of-Body Experiences

WALDO VIEIRA, M.D.

PROJECTIONS
of the
CONSCIOUSNESS

A Diary of Out-Of-Body Experiences

Translators:
Álvaro Salgado
Kevin de La Tour
Simone de La Tour

Proofreaders:
Cecilia Calderon
Pamela Hughes

Second Edition in English

RIO DE JANEIRO, RJ - BRAZIL
INTERNATIONAL INSTITUTE OF
PROJECTIOLOGY AND CONSCIENTIOLOGY
1997

Second Edition in English - 1997 - 3,000 copies.
Total of the Editions in English - 5,000 copies
Total of the Editions in Portuguese, English and Spanish - 42,000 copies

Notes: - Author's rights to this edition have been graciously transferred by the author to the International Institute of Projectiology and Conscientiology (IIPC).
     - The original pages of this edition were produced and revised using electronic desktop publishing and laser printing (text: 394,607 characters, 75,480 words, 9,763 lines and 2,608 paragraphs).

Cover: Fernando Alberto Santos

Photo: Francisco Mauro

Printing and binding: OESP Gráfica S.A.

Card Catalog Information prepared by
International Institute of Projectiology and Conscientiology (IIPC)
Center of Information and Documentation

Vieira, Waldo, 1932 -

V179p   Projections of the consciousness: a diary of out-of-body experiences / Waldo Vieira.- 2nd ed. in English - Rio de Janeiro: International Institute of Projectiology and Conscientiology, 1997.
     260 p.

     1. Projectiology 2. Consciousness and body 3. Projectability
     I. Title II. Title: A diary of out-of-body experiences.

ISBN 85-86019-25-9   CDD-133.91

International Institute of Projectiology and Conscientiology (IIPC)
R. Visconde de Pirajá, 572 / 6° andar - Ipanema - Rio de Janeiro - RJ - Brazil - CEP 22410-002
Tel.: 55-21-512-9229   -   Fax: 55-21-512-4735
Caixa Postal 70.000 - CEP 22422-970
Internet: E-mail   – iipc@ax.apc.org
     Home Pages – http://www.iipc.org.br
          – http://members.aol.com/iipnyusa/iipc.htm

TABLE OF CONTENTS

PREFACE

This book was written in 1979 and first published in Portuguese in 1981. It is now in its fourth edition in Brazil.

The facts narrated here continue to be experienced by billions of persons every night as they have since antiquity. The difference now is that the communication of these experiences is increasing with every year that passes, without the folkloric and mystical connotations which have been attached to them for thousands of years.

Conscientiology is the science that studies the consciousness[1] in a comprehensive manner, with a multidimensional perspective. Projectiology is the formal study of the projection of the consciousness (OBE). The *International Bibliography of Projectiology* contained 1,907 items in 1986. Today, in 1997, The *International Bibliography of Conscientiology* includes more than 5,100 entries.

When I wrote this book in 1979, I proposed, at the end of chapter 9, the neologism *projectiology* to name the new science that would study projection. There has been a sharp worldwide increase since 1986 in many sectors of scientific research on the 54 basic phenomena of projectiology, most notably on the Near-Death Experience. This research has served to confirm a great deal of our own findings.

As promised in the introduction of this book, we published *Projectiology: An Overview of Experiences Outside the Human Body* in 1986. This book is currently in its fifth edition (in Portuguese) in Brazil. It is a more extensive work in this area, that serves to consolidate the practical research of conscientiology.

When faced with the challenge of presenting timeless ideas and experiences in a contemporary manner, it is inevitable that a new nomenclature or vocabulary is generated. Projection is no ex-

---

[1]Translator's note: The use of "the consciousness" in the title and text of this book is a result of prolonged consideration and extensive consultation with many grammar texts, dictionaries and experts on the English language. As consciousness, in this case, is considered to be synonymous with mind, ego, spirit, soul, intelligent principle, etc., and is not being used to convey *states of consciousness*, its use before the word consciousness is considered to be appropriate.

ception. As such, the reader will find that new terms have been created in order to communicate the numerous aspects of projection as objectively and descriptively as possible. It is suggested that the reader become familiar with the glossary and, with time, the vocabulary will become easier to understand and use.

We have avoided using "spirit," "entity," "reincarnation" and other terms which we consider to be outworn, or to have religious or mystical connotations. For example: *the consciousness*, when used in the context of projectiology and conscientiology, does not imply a state of awareness or lucidity but, rather, refers to the actual soul, spirit, ego or intelligent principle.

A great number of facts and phenomena detailed in the following pages have been confirmed, amplified and clarified by occurrences during the past decade. In the period since 1981, we founded the Center of Continuous Consciousness, now deactivated. In 1988, the International Institute of Projectiology and Conscientiology (IIPC) was founded. IIPC continues to sponsor several conferences, forums and symposiums, and has confirmed the discovery of new cultural and scientific facts every year since its inception.

Reflecting the IIPC's rapid growth, our data banks show the following statistics: 1 headquarters in Rio de Janeiro and almost 60 offices throughout Brazil; international offices in Barcelona, Buenos Aires, Caracas, Lisbon, London, Miami, New York, Ottawa, and Lisbon; over 500 active collaborators; a mailing list totaling over 50,000 individuals and institutions.

Activities have been conducted in 82 cities in Brazil and other countries, 28 universities and research institutions, and 26 public and private companies, including the periodic offering of 24 regular and extracurricular courses.

IIPC has held over 20 events, including the First International Congress of Projectiology in 1990, followed by publication of the annals of the congress. In 1992 we published the *Mini-glossary of Conscientiology*. These efforts served to open the way for the practical work *700 Conscientiology Experiments*, published in 1994 in Portuguese.

According to our records, upwards of 45 institutions, besides IIPC, are currently dedicated to some type of dissemination about the phenomena of projectiology. Nevertheless, there is still much to be done to achieve universal acceptance of lucid projection and its practical applications in human life within the framework of conventional science, thus working towards a new society having transcendent ethics.

We are counting on the help of new collaborators and researchers in other areas of science to further the sciences of conscientiology and projectiology.

For all the reasons presented here, dear reader, we continue to count on your good will, good intentions, and discernment to deepen and amplify our understanding of ourselves through the conscientious and practical use of the lucid projection of the consciousness.

Let us go forth and work together, as we are now much greater in numbers, more united and cohesive, focusing on the liberating concepts of conscientiology, which guides us on the path to the maturity of the consciousness.

Waldo Vieira

CAIXA POSTAL 70.000

22422-970 - RIO DE JANEIRO - RJ - BRAZIL

Phone/Fax: (021) 247-6653

E-mail: iipc@ax.ibase.org.br

Home Page – http://www.iipc.org.br

INTRODUCTION

In deciding on the direction of this book, I was faced with three options: first, to write only about that which conforms to accepted norms of current science, thus staying within the confines of my medical training and suppressing certain information regarding extraphysical reality (as many authors have done in works which are currently in circulation). Second, to restrict and adapt myself to generally acceptable religious conditioning and profile my life as a psychic, without expressing anything new. Third, to allow myself to commit to paper whatever I have experienced and witnessed in complete frankness without repressing, censoring or offending, while remaining true to my nature and to the ambiance of the better areas of the extraphysical dimensions.

Not having anything to hide, I opted for the latter. This with the consent of the helpers (see glossary), who presented me with an irresistible suggestion: I was to obtain information, and write down everything I thought, felt, saw and remembered about the instructive excursions outside the soma. For this I would receive assistance in keeping records in order to convey the findings. I was to place primary emphasis on thinking in a disciplined way. I was to keep accurate records of the events in the first person and allow for their verification via independent studies undertaken by those open to intellectual exploration of the topic.

In order to be impartial, authentic and true to the facts, I sought to communicate the experience of the projections from a point of view in which the projector is a human laboratory, investigating its own universe, empirically but autobiographically. To accomplish this, I needed to lay bare my entire being. I used, with all sincerity, unpretentious and dispassionate language, presenting myself more as a spectator than as a protagonist, taking on the task of authenticating the extraphysical realities witnessed, stripped of any dogmatic spirit or scientific prejudice. Experiences outside the dense body are facts, regardless of how each person explains them to him or herself.

To contribute to the development of new travelers outside of the dense body, I needed to function as a reporter, fulfilling the task assigned to him. I would seek to be worthy of the trust granted to a subordinate called upon to cooperate with the purposes of service and study.

My conscience tells me that a more intense apprenticeship does not transform the imperfect, militant servant into an extraphysical traveler with an open passport to better dimensions. Just because the student chooses an exalted topic to research does not make him or her an exalted one; it only reveals his or her needs. Likewise, the fact that projection is inevitably a personal experience does not place one at a higher stage of evolution: there are myriads of schizophrenics who live semi-projected lives. Since I find myself with countless difficulties and personal shortcomings, it seemed recommendable that I do my best to settle old commitments with dignity, fulfilling my duties within the cosmoethic (extraphysical, universal principles). Hence, this volume.

Projection allows one to replace belief with knowledge. To believe in the accounts is secondary. What is important is to accept the possibility of extraphysical events. Ideally, the interested person will have his or her own experiences through training with four bodies – the soma (physical body), holo-chakra, psychosoma (extraphysical body, emotional body, astral body), and the mentalsoma (intellectual body). For this, it is necessary to discipline the memory and, above all, to sharpen one's mental concentration with a lot of willful determination, self-analysis and perseverance, by following techniques similar to those used here. After that, prepare yourself for deep renovation in all sectors of existence.

Separations from the body are experienced every day by men and women during natural sleep. Having lucid memories of extraphysical occurrences remains the most difficult, but surmountable, problem. It is hampered by the biological impediments to recall.

With practice, the extraphysical exchange allowed by conscious projection will become increasingly frequent. There will be a day when the level of awareness on Earth will reach beyond the current impossible longing to take all friends and acquaintances, one by one, to see something of the vibrating life outside of the human body. In reality, it becomes impractical, even with the use of all available dictionaries, to narrate precisely what can be perceived, thought, felt and done in somewhat evolved extraphysical environments. Projection breaks down the intraphysical barricades of the human condition.

The reader should not be surprised to find chapters containing themes rarely approached such as: self-induced projection, guided projection, cleansing projection, energetic bridge, extraphysical bait, extraphysical communicability, consciential[1] leisure, cosmoethic, silver cord, energetic cord, free consciousness, invisible unions, mental targets, mentalsoma, psychic signals, pregnant projector, super consciousness, hour of human anguish, vibrational state, and crash-projector.

New and original subjects will also be encountered such as: self-embrace, self-telekinesis, conscientiology, empty brain, extraphysical shocks, extraphysical Trendelenburg, hydromagnetic shower, in-block recollection, inverse landing, psychophonic monologue, projectiology, quintessential cord, partial projection, simulated existential series, transmental dialogue, vibratory valve, and others. *According to conscientiology, the cosmoethic is always evolving, as is everything.*

Practical and descriptive, more objective than literary, this book is composed of technical accounts of more than sixty conscious disengagements from the soma, selected from those which occurred during non-consecutive nights in the second half of 1979. Emphasis was given to those projections which offered greater evidence or clarification of multidimensionality. They ranged from the simple to the complex, from the brief to the more prolonged, from the nearby to those far away, from those of a cleansing nature to those of profound destiny, from those in which the psychosoma was used to others in which only the mentalsoma was utilized – aiming to reveal the anatomy of projection in all of its aspects, and trace the panoramic lines of exchange among the spheres of existence. During this period, there were dozens of other projections not mentioned due to insufficient data resulting from memory failures. I omitted some assisted excursions because of their similarity or repetition of topics. I deleted other projective experiences at the suggestion of the helpers for several, secondary reasons.

---

[1]consciential: of or pertaining to the consciousness (soul, spirit, essence).

Each account is divided into the following parts: the period prior to the projection of the psychosoma or the beginning of the technical record; the extraphysical period constituting the narration of the occurrences outside of the physical body; after returning, the period immediately after awakening, which I call "the technical register"; and observations made regarding the projection. The descriptions, technical records and analytic index of topics permit the interested reader to research the methods employed, to analyze and classify, and arrive at his or her own conclusions about the facts. This data may be employed for a comparative study of projections with their personal experiences or with those of a third party. In order to allow detailed examination of the projections, a certain amount of repetition in the technical records was inevitable.

Eventually, I intend to offer the public another book in which I will bring together detailed techniques and studies derived from observations made during hundreds of projections I experienced during my three most recent intensive experimental projective phases. Everything began with intermittent projections that started in 1941, at the age of nine, in a spontaneous, whirlwind projection.

I wish to express my gratitude to the helpers who co-authored this volume, particularly to Transmentor, André Luiz, Euripedes Barsanulfo, José Grosso, Aura Celeste, Aristina, Alex, Tao Mao, Maria Clara and so many others who do not wish to identify themselves. Over the course of time, they have taken me along on many assistential excursions.

Although a veteran in practice, I still consider myself to be an apprentice of projection. As such, I am likely to commit errors with respect to details which will have to be corrected later. Also, there are questions scattered throughout the text, illustrating that the extraphysical world, the consciousness and its manifestations are themes of research open to questioning and interpretation even by the most studious extraphysical consciousness[1] (chapter 32). If I may express a small wish, it is that I am able to peruse these candid notes during my next intraphysical (physical) life.

---

[1]extraphysical consciousness: someone who has discarded their soma; deceased person.

In the hope that this sincere message proves to be useful for those who research the projection of the psychosoma and mentalsoma, their relationships and consequences, I present this work – having exercised great care to ensure its accuracy. And, with the best of intentions, I dedicate this message to youths who are now becoming adults. To all those who decide to traverse the ways of projection, go my most ardent hopes of success.

Above all, I offer my most fervent and constant wish that humanity achieves, in the shortest time, the largest possible number of extraphysical consciousnesses and persons with continuous consciousness.

1. TRANSFIGURATIONS

Prior to projection

Friday, July 13, 1979. I was in the bedroom, an isolated part of my apartment on Visconde de Pirajá Street, in Ipanema, Rio de Janeiro. I regard it as the "landing field" when I travel out of the body. I use a darkening curtain in the room, which immerses the surroundings in semi-darkness, allowing me to maintain visual points of reference and get in and out of bed without losing my bearings.

After feeling prolonged pressure in the area of the solar plexus, I began preparations for a projection (out-of-body experience) under the guidance of the helpers (spirit guides). I went to bed for the second time this night at 10:16 p.m., according to the digital clock placed at the head of the bed. This, and almost all of the projections narrated here, are nocturnal due to my work schedule. I attend to intraphysical existence during the day and dedicate night life to the extraphysical dimension (non-physical dimension) as a projector. The position of the soma (physical body) on the bed was dorsal, as it will be with almost all of the experiences described here, with the head pointing towards geographical east.

Little by little, I ceased to feel the soma. The vibrational state (sensation of tingling, and pulsations throughout the soma) arrived, followed by a short period of discomfort. Removing all other ideas, I continued concentrating on saturating the mind with a single thought: a strong desire to leave and float over the soma lying on the bed. The takeoff of the psychosoma (astral body) occurred.

Extraphysical period

My intense desire to project from the soma had met with success. I was vividly aware of being in a semi-lit place, but it was nighttime. I was experiencing the sensation of being a crash-projector[1] in a large open-air amphitheater with many people scatered about. Upon leaving and floating well above the opening

---

[1] A *crash-projector* is one who leaves the soma with no destination and regains lucidity in an unknown place, among unfamiliar beings. Frequently, projections of this nature happen to beginners who project without establishing a target person, place or idea.

of the amphitheater, my presence and rapid flight caught the attention of some extraphysical consciousnesses (spirits).

A female extraphysical consciousness having unmistakable sensual intentions made a mental proposition, revealing her nude extraphysical body. I cordially withdrew, but something indefinable forced me to return to the soma. I came back to the proximity of the soma without completely reentering it and experienced vibratory sensations again, a brief period of discomfort and a new "takeoff."

I had the definite feeling of going out through the window, as the rays of the sun were shining in through the window panes in the direction of Barão da Torre Street and rising towards Corcovado mountain.

The extraphysical consciousness A. appeared. After a while I saw what looked like a lamppost and the sidewalk in front of a house. The night was clear. A. was transfigured into a dark-complexioned youth, different from the blond first-grader I had known him as. From deep within me came the intuition of the appearance of another extraphysical consciousness, a pleasant old man, deformed by an enormous semi-open tumor on his left side between the neck and shoulder. He mentally transmitted:

"Do you want to see how strong I am?"

He lunged forward, at which point I held him up with a sort of embrace. Smiling and joking, he twisted his whole extraphysical body around.

Then, two more extraphysical consciousnesses appeared, gliding down the street. As they approached, the lines of their faces grew clear. They were females of advanced age – two look-alike sisters. Through the intuition that one naturally experiences while outside the body, I knew that all three, the two sisters and the old man, were deceased Germans known by A. The locale must have been the extraphysical region over Europe. For a moment, in a sudden transfiguration, the two sisters assumed a youthful appearance. The face of one of them was covered with lesions or smallpox scars. Both were dressed in red, wearing small shawls and walked arm in arm. I asked myself: "Did they produce the transfigurations themselves, or was a helper producing the images?"

Then, still another extraphysical consciousness appeared, but it was not possible to identify it, as the call came for the long trip back to the soma and resulted in an imposed reentry into it.

After returning

Upon awakening, my hands were icy, but neither my hands nor my soma felt cold. The absence of the psychosoma from the soma had lasted more than an hour.

A strong energetic force came over me. I became passive and the extraphysical consciousness, José Grosso, transmitted audible instructions through my vocal apparatus to my wife, Elisabeth (my intraphysical assistant during my projections) about the intensification of the upcoming work, envisioning the elaboration of this book.

Observations

The extraphysical multidimensional team, composed of constantly serene, dignified and benevolent helpers, assists those while projected to perform works using ectoplasm[1]. This is similar to that which was performed during meetings in which I had participated over a long period of time at the Casa do Cinza in Uberaba (a city in the state of Minas Gerais, Brazil) more than two decades before.

The vibrational state is characterized by the movement of internal pulsating waves similar to electrical vibrations whose occurrence, frequency and intensity can be controlled at will to be fast or slow, strong or weak. These waves sweep the immobilized soma from head to hands and feet, returning to the brain in a steady cycle of a few seconds. The occurrence, at times, seems like a burning torch, surging and ebbing, or a ball of tolerable electricity guided at will. Not uncommonly, the vibrations produce a sensation of inflation common in psychophony (vocal channeling) with the apparent expansion and swelling of the hands, feet, lips, cheeks, chin and solar plexus area. The complete installation of the vibrational state is what permits a lucid takeoff and, by itself, constitutes incontestable personal evidence of the existence of the psychosoma.

---

[1]Ectoplasm - dense, semi-physical energy, that even contains a certain amount of organic substances, which can be used, among other things for phenomena involving the materialization and dematerialization of extraphysical consciousnesses and objects.

2.   M O R P H O T H O S E N E S

Prior to projection

Wednesday, July 18, 1979. I went to bed physically tired at 10:35 p.m.

Extraphysical period

I awoke outside the soma, next to a few extraphysical consciousnesses whom I had met when they had undergone a treatment program a while back. Among the five extraphysical consciousnesses, one stood out: a tall man with straight hair and an aristocratic nose, wearing a large shawl as if it were a cape.

It was clear that he was a sick male consciousness in convalescence, but endowed with an intense mental power to sculpt morphothosenes (thought-forms) which he composed and animated at will. I recognized the extraphysical consciousness to be Carnot, an eccentric friend from my childhood in Monte Carmelo, my birthplace in the state of Minas Gerais. He was there recuperating from a prolonged psychopathology by exercising the beneficial use of morphothosenes, providing entertainment for extraphysical consciousnesses needing distraction in order to help them recover. This was a leisure activity functioning in favor of evolution of the consciousness.

It was said that Carnot was a person who had gone insane due to excessive study. His eccentricities and appearance had changed a great deal. He performed a few demonstrations, using the power of thought, and appeared fully capable of performing the wonders of Mandrake the magician.

Since energy can be influenced by thought, it can be used to produce instantaneous wonders for one who is capable of controlling it. Carnot manufactured extravagant extraphysical clothes, alternately dressing himself and those present with his creations. He formed incredibly tiny objects with lightning speed. Standing before the crowd, he devised incredibly horrible as well as beautiful masks for all present, beginning with himself.

In spite of his persistent prodding, the other extraphysical consciousnesses were not able to create any objects or shapes. The process appeared to demand a lot of consciential energy (energy applied by the consciousness), concentration, quick and creative thought, practice, attention to detail and an adequate environment for the energies of the one commanding the process.

"What would the technique be to mentally create a duplicate of the psychosoma?" I wondered.

In that dimension, Carnot dominates everything. He is the ruling fish in those waters – an absolute wizard who abruptly turns the most unusual whims of the imagination into reality.

Those present did not hide their fear of his power. It was necessary to treat him like an old friend – with understanding, not fear – just like someone who visits a hospital for the mentally ill and partakes in the jokes and childish behavior of even the most mischievous resident.

With a thousand positive thoughts, I wished that Carnot would soon recuperate in order to use his fabulous mental energy in the field of human creativity.

At this point, I felt the characteristic discomfort beckoning the return to the soma.

After returning

My lucid separation from the soma had lasted more than an hour. I received no suggestion to record any of the events and the period of wakefulness seemed brief, like a simple interlude before another anticipated projection.

Observations

Following are some aspects and factors that should be observed when preparing to have a projection:

1. Bed - The projector's bed should be as comfortable, stable and quiet as possible. If one does not sleep alone it is best to use a bed that reduces interference from the movements of one's partner (squeaky springs, etc.).

2. Clock - the use of digital clock is useful for noting the time your projection began, ended and the amount of time spent outside the physical body.

3. Confidence - A positive, confident and determined attitude.

4. Doors - Make sure you will not be disturbed during the projective exercise.

5. Extraphysical patients - Extraphysical consciousnesses may be waiting in the projectarium for energy treatments from the advanced projector.

6. Family members - Try to avoid interruptions of the projective exercise by family members.

7. Flashlight - The use of a flashlight can help the projector to write down the major points of a projection after returning to the body without disturbing their (sleeping) partner.

8. Intraphysical assistance - It is useful to have someone monitor the well being of the physical body during the projective exercise.

9. Lights - Dim light (a night light, for example) can be helpful in orienting the projector when he or she is projected in the bedroom as well as upon getting up after the projection. This also reduces physical stimulus, which is counterproductive to the projective process.

10. Bedside table - A bedside table is useful for keeping such objects as paper, pencil, pen or tape recorder at hand in order to allow the projector to record extraphysical events immediately upon returning to the soma.

11. Personal hygiene - Take care of physical needs before attempting to project.

12. Nourishment - Prior to the projective exercise the projector should avoid heavy meals as well as the consumption of excessive amounts of liquids, especially those that are stimulants.

13. Nearby noises - Minimize noise. The projector may wish to turn off the telephone, intercom system, alarms, radios and TVs. Percussive noises are especially to be avoided.

14. Self-energization - working with energy exercises, especially the circulation and exteriorization of energy, serves loosen the holochakra's energetic adhesion of the soma to the psychosoma.

15. Surroundings - Familiar, comfortable surroundings facilitate projection.

16. Thosenes[1] - An individual's thosenes affect the profile and quality of the projection.

17. Visual reference points - It is helpful to have visual points of reference during the projection.

---

[1]Thosene (<u>th</u>ought + <u>sen</u>timent + <u>e</u>nergy): Unit of practical manifestation of consciousness, according to Conscientiology, which considers thought or idea, sentiment or emotion, and consciential energy to exist together inextricably.

3. A UNIQUE EDUCATIONAL INSTITUTION

Prior to projection

Thursday, July 19, 1979. One o'clock in the morning. Second sleep of the night. Continuation of the previous projection, related in chapter 2.

Extraphysical period

I became lucid upon entering into some sort of construction with a high roof and arched doors. It was an enormous educational institution. Upon going through one of the large doors, a shining extraphysical consciousness approached me, and, while staring at me, emitted this thought:

"So, do you recognize me?"

I looked at the young face of apparently thirteen years with big eyes and black skin, radiating contagious happiness. I instantly recognized him: it was Tancredo – a very sick boy whom I had treated until his inevitable biological (intraphysical) death a long time ago at my clinic in the city of Uberaba. He was one of many who I had seen and no longer remembered.

The impact of the surprise brought me uncontrollable emotion. Nothing was "said." Communication occurred through pure thought transmission. The profound satisfaction of seeing Tancredo again moved me to embrace him as I addressed the thought to him:

"Look! I'm conscious. After returning to the soma I can remember these occurrences. Isn't it marvelous?"

The flow of his thoughts returned firmly:

"Yes, it's marvelous. But take advantage of it in order to take ideas back to your physical world. Don't miss the opportunity."

Mentally, I quickly asked:

"Take what? Do you have any lessons to offer me?"

"Yes. Analyze how electronic equipment functions. It radiates waves that not only interfere with the minds of children, but also with the process of projection by affecting the vibrations in the structure of the psychosoma. Think about the effects of this radiation and their consequences."

He had not pronounced anything with his "mouth," nor had I heard words with my "ears." Sometimes, in the extraphysical dimension, the words one hears, or the thoughts one captures appear as if they were echoes. It seems that we know the extraphysical consciousness' thoughts before they are expressed. As a general rule, the projector "hears the thought" of the extraphysical consciousness in the extraphysical dimension like he "hears the voice" of a person while in the waking state.

He revealed that the institution which sheltered him belongs to the Ascensão extraphysical colony, situated on the outskirts of the city of Patrocínio, in the state of Minas Gerais, Brazil.

There were extraphysical consciousnesses in conditions similar to Tancredo's who preferred to reduce their apparent age and behave like adolescents in order to better prepare for their upcoming intraphysical life. The candidate for physical rebirth transformed not only his or her appearance but also the attitudes, interests, occupation and lifestyle, and created a likeness of the conditions he or she would soon confront. The educational institution had hundreds of extraphysical residents and welcomes visits from projected persons, utilizing their dense energies in order to give the environment even greater authenticity.

With the assistance of other extraphysical consciousnesses, Tancredo had created an environment for himself having an ambiance and installations similar to that in which he will live during his next intraphysical life. Placing himself in a sort of mini-existence, a pre-existence, or a simulated existence, he models – using morphothosenes – the same conditions that he will face in terrestrial life. It is an extraphysical setting similar to the workplace of his future profession as a research engineer in electronics.

This specialized resource of creating a simulated intraphysical reality benefits the candidates for rebirth who have personal merit and are preparing to work at specific tasks in a certain community or multidimensional team. This shows that they are doing and will do what they enjoy, having gained experience in previous intraphysical lives. They thus try, as opportunity permits, to lay a foundation in order to enrich the memory bank of the next biological body.

The process of setting up a scenario of the future, as a pre-view of the next life of the person, brought to mind the simulated voyage training of the astronauts, where each one practices wearing a specialized suit for the performance of space missions.

The higher the intraphysical evolutionary level one enjoys, the better the extraphysical conditions will have been prior to one's rebirth. On some advanced planets, the difference between the intraphysical and extraphysical dimensions can hardly be felt. This is not the case on Earth where we still confront extremely diverse conditions, not only in terms of the organism, but in the environment in which it must survive.

After a festive farewell, Tancredo left – emotionally touched by my lucid presence. As I reflected on the event, another little boy arrived carrying some kind of apparatus in his hand. He stopped in the middle of the passageway, looking like a watchman and addressed me with a sharp thought:

"Hold it there! Don't try to pass, or I will use this instrument! It can deform your face."

I sent him thoughts telling him to calm down, explaining that I was a peaceful visitor and was already leaving. I asked myself:

"Has he noticed that I am a projected person?"

Only then was it possible for me to observe the institution's surroundings. The place was an immense workshop crammed with "scrap iron," thousands of parts, sections of machines, work-benches and hanging objects, all of which were more consistent morphothosenes. Adolescent-looking extraphysical consciousnesses were practicing the mental sculpting of morphothosenes, and working with the tools and other objects they had created – learning to materialize things in preparation for their coming intraphysical life.

I did not write down the duration of this projection, which must have lasted more than an hour. The emotional impact of seeing Tancredo again triggered my precipitated return to the soma. Emotionalism generally reduces our rationality, robbing us of the ability to make serene, intelligent decisions.

After returning

An extraphysical consciousness having the appearance of a young girl informed my wife by speaking through me that, in work in which only two persons are apparent, there are many consciousnesses, including some projected individuals, actively participating in the work, depending on the night. This young girl also works at the educational institution that prepares extraphysical consciousnesses for their next intraphysical life. Later, my extraphysical friend José Grosso appeared, performed some energy exercises and departed, leaving an intense flow of energy in his wake. I immediately began to record this as well as the previous entry while fully alert in the office of my apartment. What a difference! I went to sleep so tired, roamed around and was now feeling fine!

Observations

Projections show us that one should never undervalue personal acquaintances and friendships made during human existence, no matter how insignificant they may seem. As no intelligence becomes extinct in the course of evolution, sooner or later – here in matter, or elsewhere in the extraphysical dimension – destinies will cross, renewing relationships.

4. THE OPEN WINDOW

Prior to projection

Friday, July 20, 1979. I went to bed at 10:01 p.m. It had been an atypical day with a trip to São Paulo where I had spent 5 hours waiting between shuttle flights. I was tired. In preparation for projection I emitted energy, especially from the solar plexus area.

Extraphysical period

I do not recall any details of the psychosoma taking off. I acquired lucidity in an unknown room with a half-open window. There was a man sleeping alone near the window. It was raining outside. The wind caused the window to move back and forth almost noiselessly.

Some raindrops managed to land in the dark bedroom where only a faint light entered the half-opened window. In a futile effort I tried to close the window. Even though I could feel the two bottom corners of each half of the opened window, I was not able to move, much less close, the window.

This frustrated attempt at moving physical objects while projected, in spite of the effort and will-power I used, brought me the exact notion of what an extraphysical consciousness experiences and feels when not able to contact intraphysical loved ones, due to the differences in density between dimensions.

I did not feel the presence of the helpers during takeoff. I wasn't able to gather any details on the sleeping person or his residence. I fixed most of my attention on the window in that rustic environment. Everything indicated that the helpers were assisting the possibly sick man.

After that, I felt the return to the soma and the subsequent awakening.

After returning

I looked at the clock. It was 10:36 p.m. It had rained during the day. The rain had stopped, but it was cold.

I had the clear impression that I would be able to remember the whole extraphysical visit in the morning. This is the reason why I did not immediately record the extraphysical events but left it for the morning. I later documented the projection using a small tape recorder.

Observations

With the window closing attempt, I confirmed once more the difficulty of overcoming the natural "impossibilities" of direct contact between extraphysical and intraphysical consciousnesses, and influencing objects and people while projected.

There are other simple physical actions, always problematic, which are nonetheless experiences to be attempted during projections for the personal development of the projector trying to improve his energy transmission skills.

What is the method that works best when attempting to affect the physical environment using the psychosoma? Can we pinch a friend, tickle the ear or touch someone's face, ring a doorbell, unlock a door, put out a candle, switch on a light using a light switch, switch on the TV or the radio, open a closed book, flip a page of an open book, knock on a door or tap on a table top, lift and carry a small object, open a water faucet, pull open the refrigerator door, pick up a piece of food? Which manifestation requires the least amount of energy? Switching on a flashlight with a pressure switch?

The telekinetic phenomenon is the capacity to affect physical matter by causing static objects to move and even float in mid-air. This can also be performed by a projector and thus shows the existence of a percentage of "matter" in the psychosoma. If the psychosoma were an abstract structure, empty and completely "immaterial," it would not be able to act upon dense "matter". The projector should attempt these actions when he feels the psychosoma to be in a denser state. This will facilitate contact with the object and the production of physical effects.

Repercussions or shocks to the soma during some reentries of the psychosoma constitutes further evidence of the existence of matter in the structure of the psychosoma.

5. IDEAL ASSISTANCE

Prior to projection

Tuesday, July 24, 1979. I went to bed at 8:05 p.m. Shortly after, the extraphysical consciousness José Grosso began working with energy while coupled with me. I stayed semi-conscious until 9:00 p.m. I was alone in the bedroom with the door closed.

The helper José Grosso radiated energy through me, having me sit on the bed several times. Then the team of extraphysical consciousnesses attended to someone in front and to the right of my soma.

The psychosoma is a condenser of cosmic energies (psionics in parapsychology). Emission of denser energy is used to assist psychotic post-mortems ("earth-bound spirits"; see glossary), as well as to reduce the density of the psychosoma while projected. With time, one becomes accustomed to living with both the dense soma and the subtle psychosoma.

During the semi-consciousness of the projective trance, I clearly felt an influx of energy concentrated on the right cerebral hemisphere. It involved pressure over the forehead and, after a while, it remained on the right side of my forehead only. I fell asleep after 11:15 p.m.

Extraphysical period

I became lucid outside of the soma on an unfamiliar street in a neighborhood with regular and steep streets in the north zone of Rio de Janeiro. Something told me that it was shortly after midnight. I had a clear sensation of having been peacefully left on the street.

I walked down one of the commercial avenues for quite a while, strolling among people and examining the street scenes – particularly in places with lights and small gatherings of people, like bars and nightclub entrances. I did not experience any attempt at interaction by the extraphysical pedestrians.

While passing a bar, I observed a conversation going on inside. Someone entered and bought some mint candy, which the cashier took out of a glass jar. I counted three intraphysical consciousnesses and two extraphysical consciousnesses inside the bar.

At the end of the main street in a small square with a few trees and benches, I came across an extraphysical consciousness who looked like a doctor. His name came to mind: Calmene. Strong, athletic-looking, blondish and appearing to be about forty-five years old, he was attending to some extraphysical consciousnesses needing assistance. That stretch of street seemed better lit than the others.

Upon exchanging mental messages with him, he quickly explained to me that his routine work was helping the needy. At night, the specialized task becomes intense as extraphysical consciousnesses, especially sick ones, enter into contact with sleeping persons. Each assistant in that work takes care of a defined area of service.

The traffic, except in the main street, was light. Hardly any cars passed at all. There were many cars parked in the square.

The doctor revealed plans to expand the assistance with the use of projected companions, creating a larger assistential team. This special brigade would be used for mainly nighttime assistance services in a specific place in one of the poorly lit and deserted cross streets, where their services would be centralized.

The task did not appear to be very simple. From 6:00 p.m. on – when the greatest human anguish starts – the assistential team tries to diminish the depression, despair, sadness, longings, doubts, resentments, loneliness and problems stemming from the unstructured relationships typical of big cities. He told me that the least pleasant aspect was that some intraphysical as well as extraphysical consciousnesses refused to be assisted. Sometimes, they don't even want to be approached, rejecting the extraphysical assistants. The assistance work – far more complex than it seemed – functioned by linking itself to a nucleus of police stations, emergency care units, hospitals, several temples, the Salvation Army, suicide prevention centers, Alcoholics Anonymous and other physical crisis control groups.

I deduced that such services by helpers not only existed throughout the city but in other places as well, especially in larger metropolises.

Before saying good-bye, Calmene appeared to concentrate and offered me a small message as an exercise in mental concentration, regarding ideal assistance:

"Every act of social assistance, no matter how small, signifies fraternity, is productive and deserves praise. Any kind of human assistance is better than none. Nevertheless, the ideal social assistance has its own unmistakable universalistic characteristics."

It is not official since it is spontaneous.

It is not a tax deductible donation.

It does not have a professional title.

It has no secondary or political intentions.

It does not back a personal image or cultivate myths.

It does not encourage segregation of any kind.

It is not restricted by prejudice.

It does not expect gratitude nor require public understanding.

It does not disseminate the act of assistance, regardless of circumstances.

It is the donation of one's self – simple, pure and direct – without mediation, demands or conditions. And everyone can practice it in silence.

On Earth, a planet with many countries, creatures, customs, religions and interests, all inhabitants are naturally brothers. Happy are those who learn the universalistic principle: maximize fraternity, overcome taboos and perform universalistic assistance while still in human life. In this way, they first receive the benefit of terrestrial liberation on the way to higher levels."

Could it be more logical? The message was clear, categorical and unambiguous.

I expressed my thanks and said good-bye to the attentive doctor, who left towards one of the cross streets. I walked through the lights and shadows of main street, passing idle transients and lazy extraphysical consciousnesses, and then returned immediately to the soma.

After returning

Upon awakening at 1:43 a.m., the soma was in the same position as before – the dorsal position – motionless, with arms extended and hands spread out on the legs.

6. AT THE "ATOL DAS ROCAS"

Prior to projection

Wednesday, July 25, 1979. After recording the events of the trip outside the soma in Rio de Janeiro's North Zone, I went back to bed at 3:33 a.m., lying in the prone position with the left side of my face on the pillow.

Extraphysical period

I gained awareness on an islet where a group of helpers was taking care of an extraphysical consciousness. He was sitting down and looked like a soldier with the intense stare characteristic of a psychotic post-mortem. He wore a light colored, torn shirt, and stared out over the ocean to the distant horizon. The images arising from his mind revealed the image of another soldier or sailor who had died and whom he had placed on the tip of a low rock.

The images in the demented soldier's psychosphere (aura) revealed that the right pants leg and heavy boot of his companion were hanging from the rock. The pants were made of a thick gray cloth.

On the small island, I tested my sensory inputs. I felt the cold water under the feet of my psychosoma. I heard waves breaking on the rocks and saw the tide running over the light-colored sand. The sea was bluish. The waves crashed over a small portion of the sand and rocks in a narrow spot to the left of the extraphysical consciousness who was being assisted.

One of the helpers mentally explained that the place was called the *"Atol das Rocas."* They were assisting a sick extraphysical consciousness – a prisoner of implacably fixed ideas who had been isolated on the island for a long time, still believing to be among humans. He had died during a dramatic event with a co-worker. This accounted for the vivid mental images I observed on the low rock. The ailing extraphysical consciousness was picked up by the group of helpers and taken away.

When I returned to the intraphysical base, my bedroom, I noticed that the soma was still in the prone position.

As I laid on top of the soma entering it through the back, I clearly heard a soft, peaceful voice which sounded like someone speaking through a thin tube. It was the voice of a female extraphysical consciousness. The psychosoma was still not aligned with the soma.

"Waldo! Waldo! Wake up!"

The gentle call was repeated twice, whereupon I fully reentered the soma.

After returning

In order to confirm whether or not the voice had been that of an extraphysical consciousness, I asked my wife:

"Lisa, did you call me?"

She informed me that she had not called me and, at that instant, all the memories of the events at the "*Atol das Rocas*" came rushing into my head.

I checked the clock: 4:36 a.m. I could never forget the helper's call echoing in my head like a timely alarm which did not scare me and without which I probably would not have immediately awakened or recalled the extraphysical events in this record.

Observations

To what extent did the prone position affect the difficulty of the awakening of the soma?

7. EXTRAPHYSICAL PANTOMIMES

Prior to projection

Wednesday, July 25, 1979. I went to sleep for the second time tonight at 9:05 p.m. I was sleepy as I laid down on the left side.

Extraphysical period

I became lucid in the extraphysical dimension and, soon after, I unmistakably identified the extraphysical surroundings: I was in Paris.

After performing some extraphysical assistance, the group of helpers permitted me to leave in order to make some observations for the purpose of these records.

I began the descent down a slightly inclined, tree-lined boulevard next to some parked cars.

As I glided down the sidewalk, I was thinking about having come to Paris in circumstances quite different from past trips. It was a journey far removed from what I was accustomed to, because I was traveling without the soma. I had not paid the compulsory travel tax in effect in Brazil, did not have to pay air fare, was not carrying a passport, did not have a fixed address in the city and was not carrying any money.

My thoughts attracted and inspired some extraphysical consciousnesses who were practicing the creation of morphothosenes and somehow could capture my thoughts there on the street. Were they extraphysical actors?

The group of about eight extraphysical consciousnesses, some of them playful and apparently harmless, were playing with forms that they created instantaneously. At this point, I realized that they were stopping anyone who was passing on the street to serve as protagonist in their pantomimes in that improvised arena.

One of them grabbed me as if by the collar (funny! I was dressed in shirt and coat, perhaps due to habits from prior trips) and he emitted his thoughts, with mannerisms typical of a French artist, emphatically proclaiming to the other observers:

"Look! This one here does not have documents! He doesn't exist! He came from very far away. He is clandestine! There is nothing I can do but call the Inspector."

At the same instant, another one appeared in front of me and two others behind me. They were transformed into policemen holding and pointing huge, extravagant machine guns, each one giving strict orders. They formed a circle around me and looked menacing.

I knew I had nothing to fear and that it would be better to play along, participating in the farce, while these strangers exhibited their capacity to create morphothosenes as a kind of extraphysical pastime. I was trying to keep in mind the facts that pertained to me as a character.

A fifth extraphysical consciousness dressed himself as a higher ranked policeman, came towards the others and stated:

"Hold it there! I am the inspector! I am in possession of this citizen's documents and have come on his behalf. Free him!"

From inside his huge coat, he started pulling out, one by one, an extensive collection of documents of all types, shapes and forms – constituting an enormous pile. As he continued to take documents out of his coat, more would appear from the seemingly bottomless pocket.

The spectators were delighted by the scene, although some wore expressions of fear and astonishment – not understanding the significance of the events and, perhaps, hoping not to become victims of jokes which could be played on them as well. These adults acted like adolescent students, playing practical jokes on each other. To what extent could these extraphysical consciousnesses be classified as pranksters?

Moments later, another extraphysical pedestrian caught their attention and became the center of their momentary interest. I went down the street and, after a few moments, felt the call to return to the soma.

I still had fragmentary recollections of isolated extraphysical episodes prior to this event: images of aging marks on the walls of buildings, assistance given to a projected woman and her small projected daughter who had a deep gash on the right side of her forehead, and the entrance to an old building under renovation.

After returning

In less than a minute after awakening, recollections of the main occurrences of the projection came to me in their entirety. Soon thereafter, fragmented memories of isolated episodes of other brief events which had preceded the last occurrence also returned. I checked the clock: 10:46 p.m. Paris is even further away than the *Atol das Rocas*. The tension and distention of the silver cord present important aspects for study.

Observations

Outside the soma, it is imperative to constantly police one's thoughts because they come to life, act, create and behave, as we find ourselves in an exclusively thought-based existence in which it seems possible to produce everything that the will desires. Another reason to police our thoughts is that in the extraphysical dimension they can be perceived by others in the vicinity, or even at a distance.

8 . UNEXPECTED ENCOUNTER

Prior to projection

Friday, July 28, 1979. I went to bed for the last time this night at 4:21 a.m. Before this, one of the helpers performed energy exercises while coupled to me. This had begun soon after awakening from the prior sleep and lasted for more than half an hour. I heard a rooster crow, which is a common occurrence here in Ipanema. The ambient temperature was 68°F. I lay on the right side.

Extraphysical period

I found myself outside the soma going along a road with small, primitive, rural buildings, a lot of dust and an appearance of poverty. Dawn was breaking. The inhabitants along the road were waking up and the little rustic houses were beginning to come to life. One of the houses, its front door open, had smoke coming out of the chimney. A path of beaten earth was used for the vehicles to reach the farms.

Looking at the ground, I managed to detect three slightly shining, used, Brazilian coins that stood out from the dust on the side of the road. Suddenly, I thought:

"I am outside the soma in Brazil! I need to make sure of this!"

As I scanned the area to see if anyone was there, a smiling young man appeared. I got closer to see better, and a bronzed, healthy face came into clearer view.

"Hey! It's Pinheiro!"

The extraphysical consciousness only smiled as if in agreement, but did not emit any specific thought. He seemed to be in excellent extraphysical condition.

The recollections of Pinheiro came to me in perfect detail. He was one of the brothers of a family that lived in the district of Alto de Santo Benedito, in the city of Uberaba. Pinheiro was one of the younger brothers of a friend of mine in high school.

I asked instantly:

"What? Have you already died?"

He responded clearly, in a flash of thought:

"Yes, more than five years ago."

I decided to say good-bye and terminate the mental dialogue. I thought:

"I want to remember this! I'm going to return to the soma
right now!"

Thought is living power. I simply emitted the idea and I was
instantly awake, finalizing the extraphysical experience with
a long breath.

After returning

I was still lying on the right side. The night remained dark as
the clock showed 5:12 a.m. The memories of the projection came
to me in their entirety in a pleasant manner. I felt that I had
achieved a victory by passing a difficult test with my memory.

Observations

Two facts about this projection should be clarified: I was
surprised that I could detect the coins in the dust while outside the
soma, as I have been shortsighted since adolescence; I was also
impressed by how the current inflation has undercut the worth of
small, low-value coins. How did I arrive at the road? Was it on my
own or was I moved by someone invisible to me? Could it have
been Pinheiro?

It is sometimes quite inconvenient for a projector to keep
a record of events, as it interrupts the night's rest. However, there
is no other solution, given the fleeting nature of recollection of
extraphysical events. A diary serves another important function:
the registering of extraphysical events augments the projector's
capacity for detailed observation and for the consequent transla-
tion of the experience into words. This is not an easy accomplish-
ment.

9.   TRANSMENTAL DEBATES

Prior to projection

July 29, 1979. I went to bed physically tired at 9:10 p.m. after an atypical Sunday of intense family activity with relatives from out of town. Second sleep at 12:15 a.m. on Monday, lying on the left side.

Extraphysical period

I was lucid upon entering an extraphysical institution among various candidates for rebirth who were going to be given the specific task of disseminating the principles and laws of the cosmoethic – elevated extraphysical principles.

There was a presentation of topics and debates with a small group of about fifteen extraphysical consciousnesses, whose most recent intraphysical lives apparently had taken place in different geographic areas and in various types of occupations.

I was evidently an observer, listening incidentally – a sideline spectator or apprentice, not participating directly in the work – just collecting information for the immediate entry into these projective records. Although the task of presenting these topics is immense and complex, I will try to present a few of the aspects gathered during my observations.

I did not perceive the presence of any senior expositor. It appeared to be a meeting of a study group trying to come up with common viewpoints regarding the transmission of liberating ideas during the next intraphysical life.

The main debate revolved around the traditional nature of the dissemination of spiritual ideas among people and the consequent development of prejudice, fanaticism and sectarianism.

There were two distinct teams. In each one, the leader and two other debaters stood out by their heated remarks. My arrival halfway into the debate made it impossible to capture the details of the topics, as they had been developed from the beginning. I also did not have the opportunity to be present to hear the final conclusions of the study group, if there were any.

It was obvious that one team had more rigorous and radical thoughts than the other team which was less extreme and had more liberal opinions. As our thoughts are easily perceived by others while outside the soma, my sympathy for the latter was noticed by the helper next to me.

References were made to current oriental sects, to the philosophical concepts of theosophy, to the Umbanda (Brazilian spiritual practice originating in Africa) studies and other mediumistic or trance oriented sects (including voodoo), to semi-secret organizations, to the current Kardecist (Brazilian spiritual practice founded by Allan Kardec, originating in France) bases, to the ideological assistance work based on the Gospel of Christ, performed by various religions and beliefs, to the assertions of Buddha and Mohammed, to the work of Swedenbörg as well as brief analyses of democracy and Gandhi.

Without being able to intervene, the exposure to the themes of discussion made me feel like my personal values were being held in judgment before me. This would happen with anyone there who had defined principles with respect to extraphysical life.

There was a strong consensus regarding the excessively romantic dissemination of the Gospel. Even though it was considered to be the best material available, it was not the ideal form for the dissemination of ideas on evolution of the consciousness. The repetition of ideas found in the Gospels becomes tiring and ineffective on those who are caught up in the current technological era. An approach that is not too technical, on one hand, and not too sugar-coated and watered down, on the other hand, is needed in order to motivate without imposing conditioning, prejudice and deplorable extremism that have led to many recent social calamities.

The abuse of disguised or semi-instinctive mysticism, the search for illicit and transitory enrichment and the acquisition of temporary power came to mind. All these create violence, terror, needless sacrifices, abstruse rituals and the passivity of the unwary, who follow the negative messianism of the pathological leadership of false religions, which are powered by personal interests. This instigates fanaticism, impedes public order and sacrifices consciential evolution and social progress by involving insecure, unstable and fragile humans in the clamor of group errors – as occurred in the massacre in British Guyana.

Thinking about the "conciliatory middle ground," I recalled the philosophical, moral and scientific, although shallow, principles of Allan Kardec (founder of the above mentioned Kardecist spiritual practice).

I would like to point out that between orthodoxy and universalism, I opt for the latter. Universalism is centrist and moderate, while orthodoxy is extremist and radical and as such becomes segregationist. It is foolish for one who has obtained a doctorate, to regularly belittle those who are educated by the same school.

At this point in the debate it became time for my departure, as I felt the traction of the silver cord calling me back to dense matter.

After returning

Upon awakening, I checked the clock: 1:47 a.m. The ideas of the debates I had witnessed began to gently come to mind. How good it would be if there were more physiological and extraphysical resources in the soma and psychosoma respectively, to enhance the recall of the transmental dialogues, ideas and perceptions filed deep within my memory. At times, it seems that a thick veil falls over my recollections. There is a great lack of fidelity in the intraphysical memory!

Observations

The achievement of a high degree of lucidity is the major objective in the development of the projector. Every projection causes a kind of shock to the consciousness which perturbs and confuses it. Emotionalism, euphoria, loss of lucidity, retention difficulties, incoherent interpretations, distorted perceptions and disparities in the observations of projectors occur due to this shock. For this reason, it is necessary to gradually minimize the shock to the consciousness until it is altogether eliminated.

According to the laws of projectiology, the more natural, simple and physiological the process of pure projection is, the less will be the shock to the consciousness and the greater the possibility of reaching an advanced level of extraphysical lucidity. There are external agents that can provoke projection, such as: chemicals, drugs, anesthetics, gases, physical exhaustion, hypnosis, pressure on the cervical nerves, stimulus to the balance centers of the inner ear, illness, accidents and the inhibition of desires (i.e., hunger and thirst). These provoke an impure, or artificial, projection. They are all less than ideal, because they disturb the attributes of the consciousness. They do not serve as routine, trustworthy systems with which one can acquire advanced extraphysical knowledge and perform high quality experiments.

It is thus necessary to use natural methods, discarding attitudes of extreme technicism and mysticism, as well as maintaining one's perceptions in a way that produces consistent, worthwhile results. The increased sharpness of perception outside the soma demands discipline, practice and perseverance. This allows the projector to become used to the characteristics of the free psychosoma and the extraphysical dimension, enabling mastery of one's own thoughts, emotions and energies. This will minimize the shock involved with projection, which will allow a better analysis of extraphysical events.

I propose the inevitable neologism projectiology, to name the field of *conscientiology* that studies the group of phenomena and events that comprise the experiences outside the soma – or the projections of the consciousness utilizing the psychosoma and mentalsoma.

10. IN THE PRESENCE OF EPHEMERAL FORMS

Prior to projection

Monday, July 30, 1979. Third sleep at 3:00 a.m., after registering the debates on the extraphysical themes from the previous chapter.

Extraphysical period

I was fully lucid in an extraphysical institution where the helpers projected a live scene of myself at a younger age, my mother Aristina, now an extraphysical consciousness, and my son Arthur, prior to his current intraphysical life. In order to study it, I made an attempt to approach the very realistic images without success. The ephemeral forms dispersed just like vaporous plastic, gauze, tissue or foam rubber.

Arthur was a little boy in the image. He smiled when I asked him something which I cannot now recall, perhaps due to the emotion of the unexpected, unprecedented event. As the episode proceeded, my mother embraced me, speaking affectionately and placing an aura of love around the whole scene.

It was curious that I found myself with black hair, wearing dark glasses, and extraphysical clothes – all of which were morphothosenes. It was also interesting to notice that this visual projection was not my creation, being composed of the morphothosenes of others. Had these images come from my mother? As I was thinking about it, I received an unmistakable mental confirmation that they had. The scene was from one of my projections. It had been the first extraphysical meeting with my mother since her death, an event I had not previously recalled.

Before being reborn, Arthur spent some time at the same extraphysical educational institution as Tancredo – the friend referred to in chapter three of this book. The institution is in Ascensão, located in a rural area of the city of Patrocinio, near the place where my mother passed away. This projection had occurred twelve years ago, eight years before Arthur was reborn and received that name, and in the same year of my mother's death.

The integral memory records everything experienced by the consciousness from its inception forward, detail by detail, every fraction of a second. The archives of the consciousness, while not restricted by the soma, surpass the records of the cerebral cells. And, when necessary, recollections buried deeply in the integral memory come to the surface in their integral form, piercing through the veils of forgetfulness.

During and after the brief visual projection, I maintained full awareness of the locale and perceived the presence of my mother beside me. As a result, we had a peaceful farewell.

From the institution, I attempted a direct descent to the Earth's surface in order to geographically locate the area. This brought me right over a farm. From there, I floated over wires, a slightly bent rural electricity pole, and the tops of orange trees in a small orchard.

After observing the scenery of the countryside, I thought of returning to the soma, which immediately occurred.

After returning

The clock read 4:45 a.m. when I began to record the vivid memories of my mother's presence as well as the impressive scenes from the projection, which came to me immediately in their entirety and yet gently.

Observations

The integral memory records facts in three distinct stages: the first involves a review of the scenes of events experienced during the entire intraphysical life after the passage of physical death or the "life review" or "recapitulation of memories"; the second is of the projections that occur during sleep; the third includes all occurrences in the intervals between intraphysical lives (intermissive periods). The three characters in the projection described in this chapter were in the following conditions: my mother was presented as she had been when recently deceased, my son was shown as he was when preparing to be reborn, and the image of myself was taken from a projection that I had not remembered, in 1967. In other words, the visual projection illustrated three distinct points: everything that happens to the individual is forever recorded in the integral memory of the consciousness – whether the events were experienced while in the intraphysical state, while separated from the soma during natural sleep, or while in the extraphysical condition (before and after intraphysical rebirth).

The integral memory can be consulted in whole or in part. Events which have occurred during any of the three conditions of the consciousness at any time can be shown in incredibly real form, whether in a fragmented or in-block (intact) fashion.

It is a simple case of consulting the mnemonic (memory) centers of the principal consciousnesses involved in an important event in order to obtain the complete and accurate details of the whole episode.

| 11.   V I S U A L   A C U I T Y |

Prior to projection

Thursday, August 2, 1979. Intense, preliminary exercises were initiated at 8:29 p.m., while standing up and then while sitting in bed. Upon lying down, I briefly lost lucidity. Then, I had a sharp internal mental vision of the extraphysical consciousness, José Grosso. I went to sleep at 9:21 p.m., quite relaxed, lying on the left side.

Extraphysical period

I became lucid in the final stage of the psychosoma's take-off. I exited upwards and to the right. I was certain that I was fully aware outside the soma.

The extraphysical environment was very dark, and this fact caught my attention. As I thought of dark surroundings, I began to see a bluish light. The change came not from the environment, but from the psychosoma. The artificial light that was emanating from isolated windows in houses and apartments on various floors of the surrounding buildings was stronger and clearer than the light which seemed to have appeared before me over the entire urban landscape, as a result of my expanded visual perception.

I saw a wide dirt road. I perceived an inner warning to not think about sex, as there were extraphysical consciousnesses nearby with their minds fixed on the subject, seeking encounters.

The most prominent features of the surrounding neighborhood were a building under construction and another one about six stories high already completed and inhabited. When I focused on the six-story building, the structures of the floors were visible to me, as well as the intimacy of the dwellings, as if each segment of the construction had become more clearly illuminated and more sharply focused. I could see that it was occupied. Another inner warning suggested that I should not invade the privacy of those living there.

I could distinguish between apartments with residents and others without. With omnidirectional, x-ray vision, I was seeing from a distance, around every side and in all directions at once, as well as two or three floors at a time. It was as though the skeleton of the building was illuminated and inhabited – very much like a China cabinet. With my improved visual perception, I could see the foreground in perfect focus, as well as the insides of things, without the influence of perspective. I think that this enhanced type of telescopic vision is dependent upon the density of the psychosoma, as well as the cosmoethic guiding the intentions of the individual. I do not know why, but I recalled blind projectors who see perfectly while in the extraphysical dimension.

Concentrating on one specific area, I was able to locate extraphysical consciousnesses and persons passing by, far down the street. Some of them looked like acquaintances who were temporarily outside the soma. I could see both men and women on the sidewalk. There were only extraphysical consciousnesses on the dirt road.

I examined the street, houses and pedestrians for several minutes with my visual perception which had been enhanced by the helpers. I saw no vehicles, nor could I identify the locale. As I went down the side street, I felt the irresistible call to return to the intraphysical base (location from which one projects oneself).

After returning

It was 9:56 p.m. I had spent exactly thirty-five minutes out of the soma which had continued to rest, lying on its left side. The recollections came spontaneously and naturally, as though the extraphysical events had simply been a common scene out of material life, recalled in the morning after a night of peaceful sleep. I immediately began to make note of the projection.

Observations

During sleep and even during a projection, tight clothes causing reduced blood flow, or a full bladder, and certain positions in bed sometimes provoke the erection of the penis. This event, however, has no repercussion on the psychosoma. In other words, penal erection does not occur, in this case, in the extraphysical form.

Sometimes, independent of the conditions of the human body, a latent desire or a strong impulse to have intraphysical sex during a projection can occur. Such an event must be identified, analyzed and tamed by the projector who truly desires to evolve and overcome his or her own deficiencies.

Sexual desire constitutes energy which can be vampirized by ailing extraphysical consciousnesses who can think of nothing else and live for that objective alone. These ill extraphysical consciousnesses acquire our energy through mental assaults and extraphysical attacks on the planetary crust. A normalization of one's sexual life, with a permanent partner, constitutes the only natural or physiological solution to the problem. Maintaining a singular satisfactory sex partner will serve to improve the projective processes of both.

Sexual relationships between intraphysical and extraphysical consciousnesses, or sex while outside the body, is not the same as sex while in the physical body. Orgasm cannot occur in the extraphysical dimension. What happens is that energy is exchanged between the intraphysical and extraphysical partner and the projector ends up losing far more energy than he or she gains, especially if the extraphysical sex partner is a psychotic post-mortem. The extraphysical consciousness is perfectly capable of robbing the projector of their energies – and that is typically what happens.

With this in mind, it becomes of prime importance that one's sex life (very much like one's nutritional needs) be satisfied naturally, without any fixed ideas or sentiments of guilt. The projector needs to set aside all sexual conditioning and taboos, and put his or her libido in second place. In this way, the projector is able to serenely perform other more important tasks in the extraphysical dimension.

Sex is, more than anything, in the mind. The most important sexual organ is not between the legs but between the ears. The taming of the mind constitutes the mastery of sex – and everything else. It is indispensable to know how to peacefully live with sex without placing too much value on it. Overrating sex undermines the fundamental elements of self-evolution.

We attract one another through thosenes. In much the same way that a direct evocation attracts extraphysical consciousnesses in daily life, it also attracts individuals projected during sleep. A fixed thought of sex with a specific person has the power to summon that consciousness, in certain circumstances while the soma is sleeping, for the purpose of sexual exchanges. This often causes dreams and recollections of the extraphysical events.

The above situation is commonly referred to as *congressus subtilis*. The closer the two beings are geographically, the easier it will be for the invisible union to take place. When one does not wish the union, it will not take place – irrespective of the circumstances. It is necessary to always control one's ideas and aspirations, in order to avoid undesirable approaches. Extraphysical sex can happen between intraphysical and extraphysical consciousnesses having either masculine or feminine mentalities or tendencies, regardless of their intraphysical or extraphysical appearance. Our "little venial sins" (camouflaged weak points) predispose and trigger immature behavior as well as serious conflicts.

The projector must avoid any act that invades the privacy of intraphysical consciousnesses by restraining one's unhealthy curiosity and negative intentions. This will help to ensure one's moral conduct and will maintain one's self-defense in relationships with others. It will also avoid the attraction of psychotic post-mortems who might be in the area, having been drawn to those individuals. These disturbed consciousnesses may feel that their privacy has been violated and might decide that they are justified in persecuting the projector, disturbing his or her intraphysical life and exits from the soma.

12. JAVRUS AND ORCO

Prior to projection

Sunday, August 5, 1979. I went to bed at 8:09 p.m., in a physically tired and sleepy state. I had a clear, prolonged vision of Maria Clara and was making preparations for a different type of extraphysical excursion, without receiving any details. For the projector who is being guided, the route of the projection is always a surprise. Intense energy emission exercises lasted until 8:36 p.m. I laid on the right side.

Extraphysical period

I became lucid in the extraphysical dimension in front of the extraphysical consciousness Maria Clara, who looked like an enchanting girl about nine years old with fluffy, neatly trimmed, dark hair and the appearance and behavior of a very lively child. It was the Maria Clara I already knew, but changed. She was now undergoing preparations for her next intraphysical life.

She explained that I would be making a visit to an extraphysical consciousness called Orco on my own and that I should under no circumstances be frightened, but should maintain a serene trust in the extraphysical assistance that would be present the whole time, even if it was not always visible. After that, she offered me some brief thoughts about animals and men on Earth, their tasks, evolution and their *raison d'être,* as a preparation for this projection.

The trip began in an extraphysical region bordering the surface of the planet. In a few moments, I noticed that the environment was not at all pleasant. In the dark atmosphere, the increasingly dense ambiance gradually forced me to switch from flight to gliding and finally from gliding to a slow walk until I reached a semi-dark, deserted plain. The slender threads of light that emanated from the psychosoma suddenly disappeared.

In the humid, heavy, cold environment buffeted by freezing winds and unpleasant emanations, there was only one misty light hovering above me in the leaden sky. Vague forms passed by, like obscure shadows. Strange balls of energy swirled and appeared to explode here and there. The further I advanced, the denser the air became. It was similar to the intraphysical dimension on a plain, moonless night.

Shadowy, roaming figures burst out of the darkness. They were indescribable persistent morphothosenes – some like swarms of huge delirious hornets: quick, voracious persecutors that came from all directions and which, fortunately, were chased away as soon as they appeared.

After this, there was still a long way to go. I covered the distance in such a hurry that I could not examine the surroundings in detail. An extraphysical consciousness having the appearance of a strong, upright man crossed our path. He gave me a mental explanation:

"Welcome. I am Javrus. I will introduce Orco."

I knew, instantly, that he was aware of where I came from and the purpose of my visit.

As soon as I emitted my thought, an enormous, muscular, earthen-colored mastiff, the size of a panther, having hair like a lion's mane and shining eyes that seemed human, only much more penetrating and disturbing, jumped into the middle of the winding path. He was growling with a resounding roar, like a very ferocious wolf. Sharp, pointed claws were protruding from his paws. He was a character who could impress even the most serene spectator.

Javrus made a gesture to calm him down and the hound retreated to one side, stood alert for a moment and then dove into the shadows in the same direction from where he had come.

The massive Javrus made some observations regarding the tasks he performed with Orco. He affirmed that Orco was an extraphysical guardian and should not be considered to be a regular dog, but a more evolved being with sub-human intelligence, although endowed with powerful animal magnetism. Not uncommonly, such beings are referred to as elementals or assistants of nature. Irrespective of his designation, he was a consciousness in evolution, just like any other.

He informed me that they were given many peace keeping tasks and missions of rescue and assistance to ailing consciousnesses and those still in need of human resources in order to be enlightened and rehabilitated. These consciousnesses find themselves in this state as a result of their already compromised condition and their absorption of the pathological thosenes of unaware persons on the planetary crust. Many other species of animals perform guardian duties, according to their capabilities.

He stressed that often, the person who manages to arrive at these extraphysical regions, immediately return to the soma shocked, in a state of terror and, upon initial contact with the brain, conjure incredibly elaborate nightmares of fights with monsters in implacable persecution. This is understandable since, if the surroundings and expression of Orco scare even experienced extraphysical consciousnesses having agile, lucid minds, what can be expected of persons with weak minds, who are briefly projected out of the soma in a haphazard manner, and sometimes without lucidity?

Anyone who witnesses this can understand why these scenes can induce fantastic nightmares, fantasies and mythological creations in the intraphysical mind. Duos like this must have inspired the formation of human guards accompanied by dogs which perform search, rescue and policing services.

At that point, I bid him a fraternal farewell. Javrus remained, with the abnegate mission of an incessant struggle on behalf of evolution, in an area of intense consciential conflicts. How long has this extraphysical consciousness been working there?

The departure from this ambiance was less unpleasant than my arrival, and the return to the soma occurred swiftly.

After returning

I checked the clock, after returning to the soma, which was still on the right side, and made a mental note: 9:36 p.m. It seemed that I could still see Orco's unforgettable eyes shining in the semi-darkness of the bedroom, as he advanced, growling. He stood out as the major personality in that extraphysical reality, and was now deeply etched in my memory. My recollection of Orco caused an instantaneous and complete recall of the extraphysical occurrences.

Observations

One can never stop learning. How many unknown life forms are there still to be studied! In the extraphysical dimension, we encounter more strange facts than on this planet.

The psychosoma always gives off some light, ranging from dim to exuberant. Its brightness is dependent upon the evolutionary level and condition of a consciousness and its environment. A flow of harmonizing energy seemed to ring an inner bell, prompting me to register this projection.

It is important to make a few observations regarding the sensations experienced with the energetic shower originating in the coronal-chakra (crown chakra). The willful contraction of the cranial muscles, generally at a frequency higher than the pulse and faster than 1 per second, provokes energetic detoxification which can be tame or vigorous, slow or rapid. These exercises cause yawns and tearing of the eyes and work to relieve various indispositions. Sometimes the exercise reaches a peak of acceleration after which the contractions become less intense and slower until they disappear altogether, leaving in their place a vibration that provokes immense well being. One's concentration and will-power cause the energetic shower.

Strong, accentuated energy emissions will take place during this process, which can occur anywhere, anytime or in any physical position, including in moving vehicles, as long as the circumstances allow a few minutes of isolation. During the course of the exercise, a thundering sound can occur inside the head, which is characteristic of muscular contractions, stronger than those used in yawning. This gives the sensation of having the head connected to a powerful invisible apparatus.

There is no question that the coronal-chakra plays an important role in the process of energetic detoxification as it is positioned exactly at the top of the head, radiating upwards, right in the middle of all the muscles that involve the cranium. The muscular contractions cause the moving of the eyebrows, forehead and of the whole scalp, reaching even the ears. In my personal case, I am able to easily move my ears at will.

Inspired by observations made while outside of the body, I have, through the years, used that type of energetic detoxification while I am taking a shower. This process generates a powerful hydromagnetic flow analogous to a localized, individual hydromagnetic storm and acts as a kind of preventative hydrotherapy. The water, set at a comfortable temperature, washes away the toxic energies as well as dense morphothosenes, magnetically rinsing the physical body. It has a positive effect on the aura, the silver cord and even the psychosoma. I have often observed that when there is food in the stomach, the energies stimulate digestion. Furthermore, energetic showers promote self-healing from ailments such as general physical indispositions, psychic fatigue, facial neuralgia, neck sprains and other minor afflictions. All these facts have been verified more than once.

Those who are accustomed to the use of air conditioning in hot climates and are not overly sensitive to cold air, can produce the same basic effect using an aeromagnetic refrigerating flow or, in other words, the emission of energies while standing approximately 3 feet in front of a 1 HP air conditioner installed close to the floor and set at a low temperature. This method produces indisputably positive effects. It is, however, not as efficient as the energetic action of the hydromagnetic shower described above.

Both the hydromagnetic shower and aeromagnetic refrigeration produce various positive effects which are explained in detail by projectiology.

13. ENERGIES AND PERCEPTIONS

Prior to projection

Wednesday, August 8, 1979. Time: 8:12 p.m. Phase of the moon: full at 12:22 a.m. Intensive energy emission exercises began immediately after assuming the dorsal position.

I felt a rapid movement of the right hand. This was a repercussion of the sudden return of the extraphysical hand which had been partially disengaged and had then suddenly returned to a state of alignment with the physical hand. In semi-disengagement of the bodies, this phenomenon can be called self-telekinesis when, for example, the right arm is separated while the consciousness remains awake or semi-awake, and one finger of the hand of the psychosoma touches the corresponding physical part without becoming re-aligned. When this occurs, there is a kind of harmless electric shock, quite strong and clearly perceptible, with a repercussion to the physical arm.

During the semi-disengagement of the bodies prior to complete takeoff, the last part of the soma to be projected is the head.

The soma became very numb as I turned on the left side. I experienced a brief loss of consciousness and the clear image of the extraphysical consciousness José Grosso appeared. At 8:33 p.m. the energy movement exercises finished and I went to bed lying on the left side, wishing intensely to exit and float above the soma.

Extraphysical period

After a brief period of sleep, I became fully conscious, even though I was still inside the soma. I was absolutely certain that, at that time, the psychosoma had not completely disengaged from the soma. After a short period of vibrations, I made a quick takeoff, experiencing a very pleasant sensation of freedom.

I noticed the presence of several tenuous and yet vigorous filaments coming out of my back. The filaments seemed like the type of covered wires used by power and light companies in the encasements beneath the sidewalks. They were components of the silver cord. My will to leave the soma seemed to produce a solid substance which allowed me to support an extraphysical arm and an extraphysical hand as if they were pushing the psychosoma up and out. The will acts like a lever.

A resonant thought of external origin, perceived as though I was hearing non-articulated sounds, gave a brief, slowly metered message:

"What you think of will be created and will immediately appear."

I thought about the Superman cape used by my son Arthur and a red cape appeared on my back. Looking at it during the quick flight, the cape seemed to flutter in the wind. I took a quick spin through the air and, after stopping, energy began to be emitted.

It seemed that the intensive energy exercises performed before sleeping were continuing outside the soma. The energies emitted by the consciousness together with the energy of nature, when accumulated before takeoff, assist the helpers to awaken one, to increase one's luminosity and to sharpen the visual and auditory perceptions of the projector as soon as he or she leaves the soma.

A feeling of indescribable well-being arose inside me as I glided for quite a while in the open air of Ipanema, near my apartment. The act of thinking constructively while outside the body provokes the spontaneous absorption of subtle energies from natural sources such as the ocean and forest, and permits their immediate and effective utilization. The rapid absorption of energy takes place in the same way as the reception of thoughts and suggestions from extraphysical consciousnesses.

The resonant voice warned me:

"There will be a strong noise in the vicinity of your soma, which may retract the psychosoma."

I heard the indefinable sound, and immediately returned to the proximity of the soma. What kind of physical sound might that have been? I saw my inert soma lying on its left side. I turned to match that position, and a complete alignment of the bodies occurred.

I immediately wished to return to free flight. The inexpressible freedom of flying made me feel much better than being in the soma, but a resonant thought suggested that I write down this account. I realized that the forces which link the psychosoma to the soma are the same ones that cause the vibrational state. The attraction of the soma while in close proximity to it was almost irresistible. And then, the thought of writing finally won over my momentary indecision. There was no visible extraphysical consciousness nearby.

The sensation of being in the psychosoma was still with me in the dense body. I suddenly had an idea. It would be a shame to turn on the light and disperse the accumulated energy and so, upon getting up, I decided to write down the main points of the extraphysical events in the dark.

After returning

The digital clock showed 9:36 p.m. I got up from the bed to write some notes in the dim light of the office. I filled seven sheets of paper with spaced, telegraphic phrases. As I returned to bed, I felt the general coldness of the soma.

Observations

The silver cord appears to be composed of a bundle of pulsating power cables, rather than a single cord. The distendability of the projector's energetic cord represents his "projective potential." Where is the physical attachment of the energetic cord when this appendage is retracted during landing and concealed within the soma?

The process of translocating the consciousness can be instantaneous. One can pass through the thickest sorts of material structures, however everything changes in accordance with the extraphysical dimension that you find yourself in. The denser and darker the extraphysical atmosphere is, the slower will be the velocity of flight and the greater is the will-power required for the transit of the consciousness. Local differences influence whether flight will be fast and easy or difficult and slow, according to one's will and the area's density. There are, due to the relative quality of thosenes, thick atmospheres where flight is more difficult than on the planetary crust itself. The will is the propelling agent of flight. When it so desires, the consciousness can stroll like an ordinary person or it can stop in mid-air. In subtle atmospheres, flight can reach the speed of thought, without the consciousness losing any lucidity.

It is important to note that everything that alerts the physical mind affects projection. For this reason, it is necessary to take precautions with respect to the physical base, where the soma will rest, thus protecting the projector from negative surprises and avoiding, as much as possible, external sounds and events that may interrupt the projective process or cause an unexpected return of the psychosoma.

Some especially disturbing sounds include: doorbells, telephones, intercoms, pendulums, noisy clocks, pigeons on the window sill, flushing toilets, sound equipment at high volume, noises of nearby construction, the songs of birds, vehicles crossing over metal plates, a neighborhood party, a faulty air conditioner, shaking of the floor, storms, howling winds and other natural occurrences. Background music in the *projectarium* (the physical space tailored so as to maximize projectability) is not advised.

14. FRUSTRATED VISIT

Prior to projection

Tuesday, August 14, 1979. Phase of the moon: last quarter at 4:03 p.m. I went to bed at 3:35 a.m. for my third sleep of the night, after writing for several minutes in the living room. I laid down in the dorsal position, the ideal position for projections.

Extraphysical period

I was completely awake as I respectfully entered the bedroom of R., my sister and very close friend in Minas Gerais state. I saw her sleeping peacefully, laying on her right side, with her psychosoma in alignment with her soma. She was my target person.

The suggestion came for me to awaken her without moving her soma. In this way, a transmental (telepathic) dialogue would be possible. I placed my extraphysical right hand on her left shoulder, which was facing up, and used a familiar nickname to call her.

"F!"

After employing a reasonable amount of mental force and determination with the intention of provoking her extraphysical awakening, she sleepily looked upwards seeking the direction of the call, trying to see who was bothering her.

I seized the opportunity and gave a spontaneous explanation, while taking great care not to frighten her:

"F., it's me! Look! I'm outside of the soma which is in Rio de Janeiro!"

For an instant, after giving the impression of continuing to sleep, as if somnambulant, she seemed to open her eyes and emitted a thought:

"My God! Is that you?! What happened?"

"I'm visiting. How are S. and E.J. ?"

Her perturbation by my visit was much deeper than it appeared. With a serious, younger, brighter face looking fixedly at me, she just repeated, horrified:

"No! No! Please, leave me! You must be a vampire!"

Since her emotional alteration was evident, I thought it better to leave her alone. The realignment of the bodies took place immediately and I transmitted energies to calm her.

I went to the adjoining room, gliding through the house, noticing the movement of my extraphysical arms and legs and thinking: She thinks I am a vampire, like Count Dracula. How difficult it is to make contact in these conditions! Me, a vampire, that's all I need! But her thoughts are not without reason, for they have the logic of fear.

At that point there was a noise inside of the house, coming from one of the interior bedrooms. Had my sister awakened thinking that she had had a nightmare or was another person in the house?

I had the instinctive reaction to flee and seek out a place to hide, as if I had been engaged in a reprehensible activity and was about to be caught. My thoughts caused the psychosoma to levitate towards the ceiling. From there, I could see the light from the street coming in through the tall glass windows in the living room. I had assumed that position, due to a compulsive and infantile reaction, thinking that I could perhaps remain hidden from anyone who walked in. I received an inner suggestion to return to the soma.

After returning

As I peacefully awoke, the projection felt as natural as any common event of human life. So natural had the occurrence been that, in order to test the projection, I emitted a flow of energy and noticed that the soma felt heavy. In a few seconds, I received a shower of energy. I then confirmed the presence of a helper.

As I consulted the clock, I made a mental note: 5:14 a.m.

At that moment, before beginning to write, I intentionally began to recall all of the events I had observed while outside of the soma – especially the thought about Dracula, the strange and powerful personage of Count Rochester written about by the well known Russian psychic, Wera Krijanowsky, published in Brazil as "The Hatasu Queen."

It was now 7:28 a.m. After making a long distance call, R. explained that she had been awakened at some point during the

night, but then had gone back to sleep at 4:30 a.m. when she heard
the large clock in the house striking. She was somewhat indisposed
as she was coming down with a cold. She did not dream, but said
that she slept on her right side. She always sleeps on her side;
never on her back. She also mentioned that yesterday they had
talked a lot about matters regarding us in Rio de Janeiro. She confirmed that another relative in the house wakes from time to time
through the night due to health problems and that the room has a
window which was still open at that time, near a public lamp post
on the street. She told me that she would be afraid to consciously
see me outside of the soma. She had read the novel about Rochester a long time before and frequently works with the emission of
energy, but has never seen an extraphysical consciousness and was
afraid to even think about it.

Observations

It is not recommended that the projector try to reach another
person, unduly intruding and meddling in their privacy without
consent, except in extraordinary cases like this one, based on family ties and with the intention of cooperating with lucid projectability.

15.   CLEANSING   PROJECTION

Prior to projection

Wednesday, August 15, 1979. An atypical day. Some duties and commitments required that I spend part of the afternoon and night with an amiable man I had recently met who lives outside Rio de Janeiro. The meeting had stretched out and the period of personal preparation for sleep kept me from going to bed until 10:15 p.m. The extraphysical company that had come with the visitor had stayed, perhaps to receive some fraternal thoughts. I functioned once more as extraphysical bait (a person to whom a sick extraphysical consciousness has become attached for the purpose of being treated).

Extraphysical period

Soon after the takeoff of the psychosoma, confirming the observations made before sleeping, I became lucid among psychotic post-mortems with considerable hypnotic power, wearing gloomy expressions, making threatening gestures and forming a horde of truculent persecutors.

Aware of the function for which I had been summoned, I began the treatment of these consciousnesses, in the surroundings of my own apartment, with the purpose of pacifying those classified by projectiology as *intruders*. How difficult it is when you are obliged to defend yourself!

The eight vigorous consciousnesses, having significant magnetic power, disorderly passions and a visible disposition to attack, insistently and implacably tried all they could to subjugate me. But, in my case, being a lucid projector and due to the intangible support of invisible helpers, their mental struggle became more arduous and evenly matched. Such consciousnesses always try to impede ongoing tasks and absorb the energies of those who make themselves available to them.

The helpers had apparently left me "alone" – as they sometimes supervise from a distance or are not perceived due to a difference in their frequency – in the middle of this rebellious and desperate struggle. I have participated in this sort of contest innumerable times over a long period. The dense energies of the soma make it easier to contact extraphysical consciousnesses of a low and still very material vibratory composition. The fraternal dialogue, thoughts of peace, the interaction of the helpers and the maintenance of inner tranquillity, without the emission of negative thoughts, as always, constitute the best conduct while in the middle of a torrent of energetic emissions carrying insane blasphemies and improprieties. Very often, while outside of the soma, I behave like a serene father and on other occasions, like a teacher trying to explain a simple lesson.

Only consciential authority, achieved through being a living example of what one says, allows us to have supremacy over sick extraphysical consciousnesses. Thus, the cosmoethic is clearly intertwined with the process of projection. Sick individuals make up a large part of the extraphysical population and are a burden to this school-hospital-planet. Malicious, defiant or threatening extraphysical consciousnesses only dominate those who let themselves be dominated. The cleansing projection is one of the greatest opportunities for the projector to make himself useful. Consciential authority always prevails in a high quality projection.

After a certain period of energetic confrontation, there was an increase in the pressure from the extraphysical group, with a larger number of psychotic post-mortems in bad mental conditions having been attracted by the defection of some of their companions, who had been peacefully guided away.

My mother Aristina, an extraphysical consciousness who was seen only by myself and not by the sick consciousnesses, advised me to temporarily return to the soma in order for the atmosphere to clear up a little. The intentional landing was executed with some energetic effort, since I was the target of many concentrated and imbalanced thoughts.

After returning

As I awoke, I could still feel the traces of the presence of the psychotic post-mortems. My dense soma seemed like a fortress or trench, allowing a truce in the struggle that would go on into the night on behalf of the betterment of all concerned. As I began this entry, the clock read 11:56 p.m.

Observations

The first energetic demand of this type occurred with me in adolescence. It resulted from my interaction with extraphysical intruders (malicious extraphysical consciousnesses) who were connected with a family member.

The mind-to-mind battles were like this before the current intraphysical life and will probably be so after the deactivation of the soma. The cleansing projection requires maxi-fraternity, the only resource capable of causing a great revitalization and calming those who challenge extraphysical realities in order to subjugate unwary consciousnesses, inflicting torturous suffering.

Projection is perhaps the activity best suited for the self-cleansing of any paranormal person. I suppose that extraphysical cleansing is not possible when utilizing the mentalsoma alone. During the performance of cleansing tasks, the psychosoma is always present and sometimes in a denser state in order to facilitate contact with sick extraphysical consciousnesses. When the psychosoma is within the extraphysical sphere of energy (an area of dense energy extending approximately 13 feet in all directions from the head of the individual), it increases the energetic resources available during the takeoff of the psychosoma, offering a better defense against extraphysical attacks.

As incredible as it may sound, some researchers preach that projection has latent dangers and malignant side effects such as: unbearable sensations, fainting spells, nightmares, hallucinations, emotional disturbances, hypochondria, hysteria, dizziness, migraines, panic, severe amnesia, psychic trauma, disintegration of the psyche, paralysis, cardiac arrest, aneurysm and rupture of a blood vessel, cerebral hemorrhage, morbid non-alignment of the bodies, pathological disturbances of the psychosoma, twisting or rupture of the silver cord, confused aura, violent repercussions, stigmatization, alienation from family and friends, harmful extraphysical encounters, encounters with hostile beings, accidents with the soma, intrusion, possession, death from a knife wound, occupation of the soma by an extraphysical consciousness, premature burial and physical death. Frankly, I think that these risks are greatly exaggerated and were created, in part, for the purpose of the intentional and systematic suppression of information about paranormal practices from ancient times, through the Middle Ages and lasting up until a few decades ago.

I have never identified any of these reported inconveniences as a real obstacle to projection. The obstacles that I have encountered have only contributed to the technical perfection of the projective processes, which have brought me great happiness. I find that good intentions, inner peace, constructive self-criticism, discernment and a somewhat developed projectability will naturally remove these and other, perhaps supervening, risks in some phase of the development of projection. I do not see the need for any serious restriction of the practice of projection as long as ordinary precautions are observed with respect to physical and mental hygiene.

16.   SOCIAL RECEPTION

Prior to projection

Sunday, August 19, 1979. I went to bed at 10:11 p.m. After more than one hour of preliminary energetic exercises, including the application of energy to my head, especially my eyes, I laid down to sleep on the right side.

Extraphysical period

I became vividly lucid during a classic, upwards, vertical takeoff of the psychosoma, while passing through the wall of my bedroom in the direction of Visconde de Pirajá Street, to the south.

While on the street, I saw the interior of a modern residence at a distance with a clear, telescopic vision, as though I were using a pair of zoom lenses. In the background, a distinguished looking lady attended to a little girl of school age wearing a nightgown and affectionately led her to bed.

As I observed the intimate scene, I simultaneously saw other parts of the ample house, including a spacious living room where some sort of social reception was being held.

The men and women in gala attire were moving about the room like actors on a stage, allowing me to perfectly distinguish between them and the equal number of shabbily dressed extraphysical consciousnesses of varied appearance.

I noticed various well groomed persons, some with gray hair. The majority were enjoying themselves as though they were at a party. The sounds of soft music could be heard coming from the inner rooms of the dwelling.

In no time, I entered the living room accompanying an extraphysical consciousness who gently approached another of masculine appearance looking about forty, having a goiter which enlarged the shape of his neck, giving him a disproportionate look, as though his neck and head were bigger than the rest of his humanoid constitution. My recollection of the mental dialogue is that the extraphysical consciousness refused to accompany the helper, vehemently expressing the need to stay there to transmit an important monologue to a certain person at the reception. He was, however, fraternally dissuaded from doing so. The brief, but incisive, mental dialogue involved the intercession of some extraphysical consciousnesses who were present – companions of the insistent one. After some time, he gave up and the helper led him out of the quarters along with two others who were in the house. At that point, I received a suggestion to return to the soma.

I noticed a marked difference between the clothes of the groomed and well dressed men and women participating in the reception, and the strange apparel of the extraphysical consciousnesses also present. Two of the extraphysical consciousnesses tried to approach me, upon detecting my presence as a lucid projector, but were chased away by the helper who was seen and apparently respected by all of them. The persons in the room were oblivious to the intangible scenes which were transpiring under the roof of the house, as well as the presence of a projected person whose soma was sleeping at that time. It was not possible for me to determine the locale.

After returning

Upon awakening in the soma, lying on the right side, I looked at the clock: 10:56 p.m. The events of the projection were so vivid in my mind that they still seemed to be going on before my eyes – especially the colorful vision of the occurrences from a distance, the rescue of the psychotic post-mortem and the monologue he insisted upon transmitting at any cost.

Would this have been a channeled monologue?

I got up to write the entry, in order to keep the diary of projections up-to-date.

17. LUMINOUS TOMBSTONES

Prior to projection

Thursday, August 23, 1979. Third sleep at 3:29 a.m. I laid down on the left side after having been up writing during the night.

Extraphysical period

My extraphysical awakening took place over a hill, giving me the sensation of being left in mid-air, flying under the control of my own will. I felt a deep satisfaction in flying like a birdman without a hang glider.

I noticed that it was still night and, while flying downwards in a circle over the hill, I thought of looking at my hands in order to remember having done so upon awakening. I clapped them together, allowing me to see them, light and loaded with energy, as if they contained electricity. The sensation of moving my hands was pleasant.

Suddenly, the luminosity of some bright and pretty objects on the ground caught my attention as I was coming from the side of the hill. As I descended to observe the objects more closely, their brightness increased and it was possible to identify a luminescence emanating from several tombstones. I was in a cemetery. Upon making this discovery, I had the idea of grabbing one of the ornamental pieces from a tomb; a small reclining angel which glowed like a light bulb. As soon as I thought it, the action took place. I fully experienced the sensation of feeling the object and receiving its luminescence, like "star dust" in my hands.

Finding the luminous radiation strange, an intuitive explanation came from deep within me. This was the accumulation of thosenes generated by the loved ones of the person whose soma was buried there. A similar thing occurs with images in religious temples which seem to acquire life from the intense energy imparted to them through the prayers of the faithful over time.

There are also monuments and certain statues of famous persons, whose veneration by the people transforms the objects into images similar to those in the temples, due to the positive emanations which turn into luminous energy. The essence of everything in life is thought, emotion and energy. What we think with passion, we materialize and impregnate with life, by emitting energy. The tomb, almost always an expression of human vanity, can be transformed into a repository of living forces which is what was seen on the stones of that cemetery.

My hands seemed to attract the luminescence of the object, like a magnet attracting slivers of iron, which I could touch and feel. It naturally occurred to me to compare the cemetery to a vast deposit of scrap iron.

As I floated up and away from the tombs, I saw several extraphysical consciousnesses circling a grave in a distant row. The consciousnesses I saw from a distance seemed to be working with other psychotic post-mortems, assisting those who were unconsciously still tied down to their tombs and the general area of the cemetery. There were no extraphysical consciousnesses near the luminous tombstones.

Something within me suggested that I not approach the area, as it was already time to return.

After returning

As soon as I awoke, I checked the clock: 4:14 a.m. Fragmented memories began to flow into my mind: first, the last scenes of the projection, then the luminous tombstones and, finally, the exercise of clapping my hands while flying, which provoked once again the sensation of well being until I made this entry.

Observations

The state of having the inner perceptions, intuitions, premonitions, inspirations or incontestable awareness of certain facts experienced by the consciousness liberated while outside the soma, represents impressive phenomena associated with projection. In the beginning, the projector is not concerned with their occurrence but, with repeated experiences, confidence in these processes arises and one starts to apply them rationally in extraphysical activities. It is important to stress that this condition of inner certainty with respect to the details of a fact, the mental identification of a consciousness or the clarification regarding a certain circumstance comes immediately and does not always represent the simple inspiration of the helpers, but the natural perception of the projected consciousness, a new sensorial door, superior and incomprehensible to the finite mind of the dense physical brain.

18. OPERATION EXCHANGE

Prior to projection

Tuesday, August 28, 1979. An atypical work day. I had been in the city of Niterói for a few hours. After twenty minutes of recuperative exercises, I went to bed at 7:55 p.m., in a physically tired state. Second sleep of the night without checking the clock. I laid on the left side.

Extraphysical period

I awakened in the extraphysical dimension as I was entering an institution of multidimensional studies on a small deserted island. I was among various persons projected outside the soma, assisted by a team of helpers, all led by an instructor.

The projected persons were congregated as they arrived, each one accompanied by an extraphysical consciousness. They were treated with energies in the area of the head, in order to increase their lucidity and improve their reasoning capacities, thus facilitating more precise recollections after the extraphysical excursion.

The place, managed by a sizable team, functioned as an improvised establishment, but possessed authentic educational resources as in universities on Earth. According to explanations provided at the time, everything possible had been done to make the recent arrivals "feel at home." This would predispose their enhanced lucidity while outside the soma, which would allow the assimilation and later recollection of extraphysical events in a somewhat integral form – generally in the form of intuition or dreams.

The operation was performed on an island in order to facilitate the transportation of the projected persons as well as the consolidation of the extraphysical defenses of the environment. I could see that the area was completely isolated by light strips, creating a campus-in-the-wild environment among the trees and over the rocks of the island.

In the installation, there were desks placed in rows, pictures on a wall, a simple podium at an elevated point and a place like a screen for projecting visual images, situated directly in front of the seminar leader.

There must have been more than four dozen projected men and women including some youths, authorities, public servants, teachers, medical staff and participants belonging to various religious groups. Some knew each other and formed small groups.

As they began the exposition of what they called "operation interchange", a series of luminous, three-dimensional maps and graphs of a determinate area was shown – each one dealing with a particular aspect of human life and all dealing with the same geographical area which seemed to be a particular neighborhood of the city.

Then, short lectures were given by three different extraphysical consciousnesses, developing the purpose of the meeting. They explained that, after small consecutive classes, an instructor would listen to the opinion of each one of the persons who were temporarily liberated through physical sleep.

The work entailed quick and intensive preparation for extraphysical assistance in a particular area of the city where the participating persons were from, each one currently living in the area under study and possessing a different knowledge and responsibility. They informed me that similar teams are common in the extraphysical world, scattered throughout almost all countries on various continents. Out of these programs have come the ideas that have inspired intelligent assistance along the lines of "Operation Rondon," conducted in Brazil, "Operation Clean-up," undertaken in slums, and other related undertakings in which hundreds of residents of specific zones are assisted by all available emergency resources.

In this case, the participants of the educational activity were being brought together to enact a broad collective task of extraphysical cleansing, with the hope of improving the condition of and even, in some cases, rescuing intraphysical and extraphysical consciousnesses.

The hosts of the event stated that the cleansing being done is still very elementary in view of the real needs of those being assisted. These consciousnesses live in situations of group and reciprocal energetic parasitism wherein extraphysical consciousnesses try to force temporary, artificial, semi-physical lives and transmit pathological energy emissions through processes of intrusion and energetic drainage of their intraphysical hosts.

The presentations were very intelligent. They dealt with the issues of family and community life and sought to introduce simple, renovating concepts related to all aspects of human existence in a very natural and friendly way, free of mysticism or prejudice. They were presented in the manner of university students at ease on campus.

The basic concept of the cosmoethic stood out in all subjects addressed and was discussed in an impartial, universal way, uniting consciousnesses of all backgrounds, ideologies and religious beliefs.

A great range of topics was covered, including domestic life, work, transportation, health, leisure, school and survival. All of them, however, converged on the same point: the co-existence of intraphysical and extraphysical consciousnesses in homes and community centers such as clubs, associations, large and medium size companies, fitness classes, and meetings of various types including religious, political and union gatherings.

The themes of discussion brought to mind, in a general way, the clean-ups performed by police, the collection of vagrants before public celebrations and preparation of public places for inaugurations or solemn acts commemorating important community events.

After informal, unspoken explanations were instantaneously transmitted, the instructor arrived. He was a luminous, radiantly pleasant extraphysical consciousness who presented the final part and conclusion, beginning by questioning each one of those present about the operation and listening to their suggestions.

The majority remained awake and answered the questions, effectively participating in the meeting, giving opinions and making suggestions. However, some of them, including two projected men and a projected woman, fell into a continuous sleep and were not able to participate in the mental dialogues. They were isolated before being returned to their physical bodies, an event that occurred simultaneously for dozens of projected consciousnesses who left in a single cluster at the end of the meeting with a prognosis of peace.

The meeting served as proof to those present of the efforts and abnegation of the extraphysical consciousnesses assisting men and women throughout the Earth. These helpers work to improve the conditions of life for those persons on the path of self-improvement, increased fraternity, deep community spirit and a greater sense of humanity.

What a great deal of work still awaits those who are open to fraternal participation! At first sight, the tasks appear to be performed by veterans who are dealing with complete novices. But a joint effort is always fruitful, and that is what they emphasized. The sketchy ideas in the unconscious end up germinating in the more capable minds in the community as vague intuitions and inspirations of imprecise origin which are then implemented in daily life. These ideas often appear to be rough parodies from an extraphysical perspective, but are perceived to be legitimate and practically spontaneous by those receiving the information.

Upon leaving the locale, the islet seemed to me to be covered by luminous signs, taking on the qualities of a majestic pyrotechnic spectacle, the entire oblong hill being covered with sparkling lights.

After returning

When I awoke in the soma, the clock read thirteen minutes past midnight. How long had the meeting lasted? It is difficult to know precisely.

Observations

Time outside the soma is always an enigma, a mysterious and perplexing dimension, becoming quite relative and even seeming to stop at times. Time is an intraphysical tool of measurement. With physical death, only time and the soma die. Those who experience biological death, according to their condition and the extraphysical body used, live without a future, or within a space-time continuum, if they wish.

Following are some basic differences between dreams and projections:

1) Ordinary mental activity is experienced in a dream: in a projection, mental activity can transcend the richness of the waking state.

2) During the dream state, one's reasoning capacity is diminished; in a projection, the intellectual capacity is equal to and commonly surpasses that which is available to us in the ordinary waking state.

3) In a dream, a person maintains the role of a passive spectator of events; in a projection, the projector takes an active role in unfolding events and has decision making abilities equal to those of waking life.

4) In a dream, one accepts as natural the most absurd occurrences through lack of lucidity; in a conscious projection, critical judgment is always operative.

5) In a dream, one does not maintain a sequential memory of images; the lucid projector can remember events of a projection in their entirety, down to the smallest details.

6) A self-hypnotic suggestion will not effect the coordination of dream events and images; the same suggestion can have an influence on extraphysical events.

7) One does not begin dreaming in the waking state; in a projection, it is possible to maintain lucidity before, during and after the projective process.

8) In a dream, there is no impression of a takeoff from the soma; in a conscious projection, the takeoff experience is fascinating and unique.

9) It is very difficult to prolong a dream; it is possible to prolong the stay outside the soma.

10) In a dream, sensory excitement results in the production of fantasies; in a conscious projection, touching the immobilized soma even lightly causes the return of the psychosoma to the soma with the unmistakable sensation of the traction of the silver cord.

11) A dream does not include the number of psychological and extraphysical factors common to projection, such as the high degree of lucidity, the sensation of freedom and well-being, mental clarity, expansion of capacities, gliding, flight and, sometimes, even euphoria.

12) In a dream, images are deformed and unreal; in a conscious projection, images do not become deformed.

13) In a dream, images are weaker than those perceived while in the waking state; in a conscious projection, they reach the highest intensity of any state of consciousness.

14) Dreams, although having weaker images, are easier to remember, as they occur in a state of consciousness in which the psychosoma is either almost in alignment with or is at least in proximity with the soma; a conscious projection, while its images are more intense, is more difficult to remember, as projection occurs at a distance from the soma. Thus, it is not directly influenced by the physical brain. This is one of the most noticeable paradoxes of projection: the more prolonged and distant the excursion of the psychosoma or the mentalsoma, the more difficult it will be to remember.

19. THE NEW EXTRAPHYSICAL CONSCIOUSNESS

Prior to projection

Tuesday, September 4, 1979. Third sleep at 3:55 a.m. I laid down on the right side.

Extraphysical period

I became lucid in an extraphysical institution with a very pleasant environment whose interior, being some twenty feet high with broad doors and windows, was worthy of note.

Various groups of extraphysical consciousnesses were situated in comfortable places and, in one of the delightful large halls, some of them were stretched out on beds. My attention turned to a kind, young looking, sexagenarian, bald male with a deep wrinkle of attention between his eyebrows. He was settled on a bed next to another male of advanced age who was at the head of his bed. I received a mental explanation that this had been his father.

The sexagenarian had recently become an extraphysical consciousness (had passed through biological death) and was already aware of his situation, according to the mental transmission that occurred between the two. The light complexion of the extraphysical novice was glowing with happiness and euphoria contained only now and then by the father, who was trying to make him comfortable in bed, by laying him back against a voluminous pile of pillows. My presence was not noticed by them as they had just met and were enthusiastically catching up on things, as one would expect from two relatives seeing each other after a longer absence. I asked myself if I was projected in the mentalsoma.

The newly arrived extraphysical consciousness seemed to be in excellent condition, as indicated by the satisfaction evidenced in the meeting. I was trying to understand the exceptional height of the institution's interior space. Could it serve to calm the recent arrivals from terrestrial life, illustrating the insignificance of the intraphysical dimension compared to extraphysical greatness? Or was it a result of my extraphysical visual perception?

At this point, I saw another extraphysical consciousness, an ecstatic male who had entered the quarters through one of the wide side doors, having come to welcome the recent arrival. Concentrating all my attention, I clearly noticed that the extraphysical consciousness emitted a barrage of affectionate and absurd swear words in his transmental dialogue, out of habit from terrestrial life. The two joyfully celebrated the visit, as both had perhaps previously done during their intraphysical existence.

With a juvenile excitement reigning over the reunion, they embraced exuberantly, expressing jubilation and mutual declarations of friendship under the calm observation of the father at the bedside.

I began to reflect on the spontaneity of the scene: the loving, seemingly boundless outpouring of so many "audible" swear words in that elevated environment, the authenticity of the extraphysical consciousnesses' behavior and its consistency with their previous intraphysical lives. Thoughts and acts occur simultaneously in the extraphysical dimension.

Returning to the immediate vicinity of the soma, I unexpectedly experienced an unpleasant sensation. The realignment of the psychosoma with the soma then occurred within a few seconds.

After returning

I immediately opened my eyes and found the cause of the discomfort and subsequent call to return to the soma. The right arm had been in an uncomfortable position, resulting in poor blood circulation. After trying, for a few minutes, to improve the circulation in my arm, I checked the clock. It was 4:49 a.m. It was getting brighter outside and I could hear some birds chirping.

Observations

The mentalsoma can act, isolated and independent of the psychosoma. We consider that the intraphysical consciousness has a set of bodies (holosoma) composed of the soma, holo-chakra, the psychosoma and the mentalsoma. In addition, the consciousness can project a portion of the holo-chakra. The consciousness also presents the energetic connections of the silver cord and golden cord. I consider the other "bodies" mentioned in the ancient texts and Theosophy to be referring to different *states* of consciousness.

It is interesting to note that, even though I had indeed been projected in the mentalsoma, having left the psychosoma inside the human body, I had experienced projective repercussions from the physiological problem of poor circulation in the right arm.

An extraphysical consciousness of average evolutionary stature, when asleep in the extraphysical dimension, leaves the psychosoma at rest and visits other dimensions using only the mentalsoma. Such actions constitute their mental projections, lucid dreams and lucid projections. To a certain extent, the advanced projector can do the same. He or she can extract the psychosoma from the soma, leave the psychosoma at rest in the extraphysical dimension and then project from there using the mentalsoma as if he or she were an extraphysical consciousness. In this way, the projector has the advantage of maximizing his perceptions while outside the intraphysical dimension. Is it not strange that the consciousness is capable of temporarily maintaining two inanimate vehicles simultaneously? The mentalsoma, beyond being the seat of the consciousness, shows itself to be a more flexible and efficient vehicle than the psychosoma for the transport of the consciousness.

20. HYDROMAGNETIC STORM

Prior to projection

Thursday, September 6, 1979. Phase of the moon: Full at 8:00 p.m. I went to bed at 8:08 p.m. upon sensing the presence of some extraphysical consciousnesses that were in attendance for the night's tasks. The ambient temperature must have been about 68°F. I laid down in the dorsal position with a pillow under the right knee, another under the left arm, and a thin bed spread and blanket pulled up to my chin. No energy exercises occurred. There was only time for some brief concentration and communication with the helpers.

Extraphysical period

I experienced an immediate projection and fully awoke in the company of two extraphysical consciousnesses who were friends of mine. One of the helpers was Aura Celeste, a benefactor and highly evolved companion. The helpers immediately informed me that the purpose of this trip was to retrieve a sick female extraphysical consciousness.

After traveling rapidly for a few minutes, we arrived at a deserted coastline of the continent being battered by a mighty storm of lightning flashes, thunder clashes and heavy showers in foamy swirls. The storm seemed, at that moment, to be at its peak.

The helpers informed me that, as well as there being a physical tempest, there was a torrential rain of magnetic energy falling that emanated from the higher spheres in that region. This energetic storm was aimed at the periodic cleansing of dense morphothosenes in the subterranean caverns.

The storm was like a massive earthquake and seaquake combined, stirring up immense waves, heaving up the soil and shaking the structures of the whole scene. The caverns began to get inundated by underground rivers, forcing the evacuation of resident animals, including rats running from their dens, fleeing sea otters with eyes shimmering in the darkness, and bats darting wildly through the air. All were in a panic trying to escape through the numerous caverns, precipices, and gashes that penetrated the depths of the terrestrial mass.

We glided over the elements, using our maximum level of deep inner forces in order to float over the hordes of animals and through the swarms of bats.

The icy environment in the fume-filled caverns, disclosed a magnificent and horrid beauty surpassing any nightmare. Between the colors of the jagged rock walls and the static majesty of the stalactites and stalagmites, numerous bands of suffering extraphysical consciousnesses – mentally alienated, without human bodies, but still extremely dense and feeling the magnetic effects of the tempestuous convulsions of the elements – ran, horrified, through the natural labyrinths in a depressing and terrifying "save yourself" state.

The enclosures of the caverns seemed transformed into catacombs of horror. Anguished dread showed in the appearances and gestures of the unfortunates who were gathering wherever they could. Disturbed, often dumbfounded and sometimes shaking extraphysical consciousnesses desperately sought support amongst themselves.

A deep, spontaneous compassion arose in all of us witnessing the unforgettable scenes. We tried to remain floating in the difficult position of impotent spectators before the realism of the programmed catastrophe. We controlled our emotions and stifled our impulse to weep convulsively.

Sections of the suspended geological elements shook loose and plummeted into the swirling waters of the spacious grottos that had sheltered a considerable extraphysical population. The extraphysical consciousnesses were now floating in the mixed rain and sea waters, having emerged from hidden dungeons and prison-cell-like mud holes that were tucked away in concealed places, in one of the worst atmospheres imaginable.

Waves of small luminescent teams of extraphysical consciousnesses – agents of the consolation task (see glossary) – were arriving to perform works of fraternal assistance during and after the hydromagnetic storm.

As the last effects of the storm passed, the helpers took advantage of a period of calmness to make an approach. Upon finding the small, sick female they were looking for, they took her with unsurpassable zeal from one of the indescribable refuges situated in the perennial shadows of the most twisted recesses of deeply entrenched gutters, gorges and troughs.

The deformed, squalid creature gave the impression of mental deficiency, immersed in a dark night of idiocy behind glassy eyes. She was totally oblivious to the storm's occurrence, as if living in her own world of endless nightmare.

As a projector, I functioned as a common donor of energies. A tiny group of unbalanced extraphysical consciousnesses tried to prevent the rescue of the sick little female who was now sleeping. This group of detractors was dissuaded by the energetic defenses established with the *thosenes* of the rescue team.

During the last phase of the rescue mission, when I was leaving the locale together with the two helpers and the extraphysical child, loud complaints and protests could be heard from the horrid extraphysical consciousnesses who remained and were beginning to celebrate the end of the storm in a bizarre orgy, loudly reciting pornographic verses by Bocage[1].

Our departure from that environment after the storm was quick and easy. One of the extraphysical companions, with exuberant good will, took charge of the sick little female. It was time to return to the soma.

After returning

Upon awakening, still with the vivid images of the storm, the rats, the otters and bats, my brain translated the faint echoes of the inexpressible sensations I had experienced only moments before.

The soma was still in the same peaceful dorsal position. I checked the clock. It was 9:51 p.m. The projection had lasted one hour and forty minutes. I felt a powerful energy and the extraphysical consciousness Aura Celeste arrived. I vocally channeled her fraternal instructions to my wife who had just entered the room to sleep. After the message was delivered, I began to write this entry in the office of the apartment. The weather in Ipanema was still good.

---

[1]Manuel Maria Barbosa du Bocage: Portuguese poet, 1765-1805.

21. MADONNA AND CHILD

Prior to projection

Sunday, September 9, 1979. At 8:35 p.m. I laid down on the left side, after contemplating various matters since 7:09 p.m. After checking the clock, the vibrations increased. I tried to take off without success.

Extraphysical period

On the second attempt, I turned the psychosoma to the right, exited, stood up on the bed and saw the extraphysical consciousness Aristina, my mother, who gave me an emotional embrace. I could clearly see her face and commented:

"You are younger and more beautiful. You look like you did in that picture in the photography drawer. Your face is a little fuller."

She smiled and made a reference to my son Arthur who was sleeping in the next bedroom, which is situated between my bedroom and the office at the other end of the corridor. As I spoke about him, I felt the impulse to see him. He was now my target person. I immediately found myself at his bedside where, with Aristina's help, it was possible to pick him up in his psychosoma.

Under Aristina's kind gaze, the little one became conscious and I asked him if he wished to see how the sky rocket, that we had talked about before going to sleep, flies. He expressed the desire to try. I made a quick ascent into the open night air holding Arthur in my arms. After flying up and down and back and forth in all directions over the ocean all the way to Two Brothers hill with the boy radiant with joy, I made a temporary landing at one of the entrances of the unfinished construction of the Panorama Palace Hotel on the side of a nearby hill.

I was examining Arthur, who was nude, by passing my hand over his back and body, when a youthful extraphysical male suddenly appeared, wishing to play with Arthur.

Upon calmly asking this extraphysical consciousness to go away, he leaped with one jump over the half-wall of the construction's frame, disappearing into the night in the direction of the neighboring slum. Arthur was more or less lucid, but kept his childlike mentality.

In a few seconds I returned to the apartment, leading Arthur towards his soma in his bedroom. I no longer saw Aristina. I felt vibrations indicating the presence of my dense body and, just as metal shavings are attracted by a magnet, the psychosoma returned to the soma and I awakened.

After returning

Upon pressing down on the clock, the luminous indicator read 8:52 p.m. I hesitated a few minutes over whether or not to register the preceding events, thinking about the clarity of awareness before, during and after the projection. Then, I visited the bedroom of the boy and saw him resting peacefully. I searched the drawer with the photos to find the picture of Aristina taken in 1930, and confirmed the physical likeness. Elisabeth was in the living room watching television. She told me that she had last checked on Arthur at about 8:10 p.m. Arthur was now fast asleep.

Unfortunately, due to the very personal nature of projection, it is not always possible to avoid boring the reader with family stories. What can I do?

Observations

My initial preparations for a projection, in this case from the dorsal position, usually follow this sequence:

1. Place the feet apart from each other, letting the soma relax totally with all parts in comfortable positions.

2. Rest the extended arms with hands open along the side of the soma or over the legs, without crossing them.

3. Place the head in a position which does not stress the neck.

4. Maintain the face free of muscular contractions.

5. Close the eyelids, as if to sleep.

6. Avoid the swallowing of saliva or the forceful respiration of air through the nose.

7. Through relaxation and without moving even a finger, reach a state of complete immobility or semi-lethargy.

8. Bit by bit, mentally cease to feel the soma, imagining that it no longer exists.

9. Have peaceful thoughts focused on the act of projecting, imagining the departure of the psychosoma from the soma.

10. Intensely wish to float over the soma or to roll the psychosoma to one side, depending on your preference at the moment.

22. COSMIC COMMUNICATION

Prior to projection

Sunday, September 9, 1979. Second sleep at 10:22 p.m. After registering the projection related in the last chapter, I laid down on the right side.

Extraphysical period

Following a helper, we visited the house of a psychic who works in a center on the same block near his residence. We checked on the possibility of the medium accompanying us outside the soma on a visit we were about to make to the center where he works. We discovered that it would be impossible due to the physical and psychological conditions of the gentleman at the time, as he was still awake and busy with some household tasks. Does this kind of situation occur frequently?

As we turned at the end of the block, after leaving the simple residence, we faced the closed entrance doors of a spiritist center which, from the street, appeared to be dark inside. We entered through the door next to the table from which meetings were directed. The scene in the main hall was touching and appalling. More than two hundred sick extraphysical consciousnesses, in the worst conditions, were being treated by male and female extraphysical consciousnesses dressed like nurses. In order for the sick to receive the benefit of energetic treatments, the nurses accommodated them, in their promiscuity, clamor and deplorable disorder, as best they could. There were only a few persons temporarily projected from the soma in a silent group. They were withdrawn and, by all indications, praying along with the directors of the work. There were a few simply dressed females of humble origin in this group.

Upon being led to the table by the helper, I was able to hear, then and there, some statements made by an intangible consciousness who temporarily coupled with my psychosoma. Helped by the concentration of the extraphysical team and the projectors, he semi-materialized himself in front of those present.

Various groups of the sick consciousnesses backed away stunned, kneeling down, hiding their faces with their hands or putting their arms over their heads as if surprised by the apparition or afraid of the power emanating from the visitor. The cosmic communication that this extraphysical consciousness made began with firm reference to God's mercy. It lasted perhaps an hour, not permitting me to catch the ideas due to my semi-lucid condition at the time. I perceived, however, that the extremely potent mental emissions, made up of deeply realistic mental constructions and a substantial energetic magnetism, were succeeding, little by little, in pacifying the wild, unstable crowd.

Upon concluding a prayer in that environment full of suffering, the extraphysical consciousness, already entirely tangible, went to assist isolated cases, together with the extraphysical directors of that night's tasks in the spacious spiritist center.

I cannot forget the painful vision of the abnormal faces of the sick consciousnesses who were assisted. Especially one case which the circumstances allowed me to better observe. The extraphysical consciousness had been a woman about four-and-one-half feet tall, deformed and demented, with a massive abdomen, slender crooked legs and, in the middle of her grimy forehead, above the nose, an enormous, striking, singular, endlessly tearing eye. She was totally disturbed by the mental suffering caused by the sick environment's hypnotic effect. Putrid, fetid odors emanated from the sick woman, agitated by overlapping convulsions, instilling pity and repugnance.

After attending the female cyclops, who immobilized herself as if anesthetized, the extraphysical consciousness assisted a few psychotic post-mortems, bid farewell to everyone and dematerialized. The room was now a bit more orderly and tranquil.

The extraphysical nurses began to leave with their patients. In a short while, the center's environment would once again assume its usual characteristics.

Still accompanying the helper, I left the locale to return to the physical base.

After returning

The clock read fourteen minutes past midnight. The memories came back to me quickly and, with them, the irresistible suggestion to immediately write down the painful scenes witnessed during my almost two hours of absence. The soma felt similar to heavy clothing, like a heavy overcoat with its pockets stuffed with lead.

Observations

It is common for helpers to take advantage of available physical surroundings such as empty centers and churches when they are closed. There they hold assistance meetings for those in need, utilizing the energies in these locales, which are built for that purpose. Many intraphysical attendants are requisitioned outside the soma to collaborate in such works.

23. *EXTRAPHYSICAL SELF-EXAMINATION*

Prior to projection

Wednesday, September 12, 1979. 8:35 p.m. I laid down on the right side for a second sleep. Bedroom temperature: 80.6°F. Good weather. I had gone to bed physically tired and sleepy at 7:43 p.m., after a day of intense work.

Extraphysical period

I remained alert for a long time until the takeoff process serenely began. When I left the soma, standing over the bed, I gave a vigorous yank forwards and upwards, exiting in the direction of the window. I flew like a pilot ejected from the cockpit of his plane. It is like that. Sometimes, in takeoff, the psychosoma seems to have a certain power of ejection. It was not just an instantaneous projection. It was an "extraphysical escape".

The satisfaction of relaxing once more in free flight, away from material limitations and the influence of gravity was marvelous, perhaps due to my fatigued state when I had gone to bed. The state of expansion, plenitude and freedom outside the soma brought me indescribable pleasure. How I wish at moments like these to contaminate others with this joy! I wish I could talk over every loud speaker, radio and television station to the whole world and tell them about this practical resource to achieve absolute inner peace that is within everyone's reach. I wish I could let all my friends and acquaintances feel this extraordinary condition of the expansion of the consciousness beyond dense matter!

Feeling extremely light and free in mid-air, I exulted over the thought of remaining in the soma on Earth. The gratifying possibility of flying filled me with a profound desire to offer myself as a genuine element of assistance to suffering and ailing consciousnesses, to be constructively productive in the extraphysical dimension, to somehow live up to the privilege of this liberation and ecstasy which repeats itself with each projection into space, into the ether, into the infinite, into All.

In open space over the Atlantic Ocean, with the flowing movements of free flight, in a spontaneous choreography,

I "danced" and "sang" a deeply felt thankfulness for the opportunity of being, albeit temporarily, lucid outside the dense body. As I had done in earlier similar instances, the act of thanking the multi-dimensional helpers tamed the counter-productive euphoria, returning me to a state of balance, self-criticism and mental serenity.

I did not notice the presence of any helper, but felt the overwhelming, resonating inspiration to verify the "morphological" or "anatomical" condition of my psychosoma. This was my target idea. Stopping in open space, I passed the right hand over the left shoulder confirming the presence of a dark, hairy birthmark or my "factory trademark" as they used to kid me during my childhood, being about 2.5" long and 0.75" wide, located on the left deltoid. This observation did not surprise me, as I had already verified its presence over a decade ago.

The myopia I have had since adolescence, the permanent buzz in the left ear and the "scraping" sound created by the narrowing of the space between three cervical vertebrae upon moving my head from side to side that have been with me since an auto accident in 1970, completely disappeared while outside the soma – facts I had observed before, even during partial projections.

Thoughts condition the characteristics of the psychosoma which determines the form of the soma within biological laws from conception. The soma is a replica of the psychosoma down to the smallest detail, including pores, fingerprints and hair.

As I considered that I was dressed in the pajamas in which I had gone to bed, I touched my thorax and arms, and confirmed the thought. Next, after arriving in my bedroom, I performed an inspection along the lines of a clinical physical examination, attesting to the presence of the navel and all external anatomical parts, including facial features and genital organs.

To conclude the "physical" inspection of the psychosoma, I raised the right hand to my back, head and neck, and once again very closely examined the "skin" of the neck region and the silver cord. It again impressed me as being a combination of tiny, loose cords or fine, occasionally sparkling elastic strings, firmly attached to the psychosoma. The silver cord exhibits warmth, flexibility and the texture of human tissue. It has a structure and nature closer to that of the psychosoma than to that of the soma. The energetic filament does not seem to stop at the skin. It gives the impression of entering the soma and establishing a deep connection with one or more vital centers. Could one of them be the pineal gland? How can such an apparently fragile structure have such a powerful flow of energy?

While I deeply pondered the fact, as if engaged in an internal monologue, I held the silver cord close to the soma and activated the return system by pulling on this appendage. In seconds, I was consciously "diving" into the physical body.

After returning

My awakening was spontaneous. I had not suffered any lapse in lucidity when returning to the body. The soma remained on the right side. The clock read 9:48 p.m.

When I left the bed to write down these notes, the soma seemed to emit vital energy like a big burning fuse emitting sparks wherever I passed.

Observations

Frequently, a state of tiredness and drowsiness predisposes the soma towards a temporary liberation of the psychosoma. This occurs because the cardiac rhythm slows down and allows the relaxation necessary for a voluntary projection.

An effusive sense of satisfaction, in the same way that it provokes a temporary loss of the ability to reason, causes the projector outside the soma to lose the calm needed to maintain a "peaceful coexistence" with the silver cord. The projector must fight against euphoria so that the mind can utilize its ability to perceive events and make coherent decisions.

The psychosoma is the director of the form of the soma within the parameters of biological, and especially genetic, laws. This is why the projector encounters it in the extraphysical realm as a true twin of the soma in every microscopic detail. However, it is the consciousness that controls all of this. In other words, the soma is guided by the mentalsoma, the seat of the consciousness, which respects the actions of biological laws. In the case of identical twins, for example, it is not that these relatives are beings of identical levels, evolutionary characters and psychosomas, but rather, they are different extraphysical consciousnesses who are reborn along similar morphological lines, organized according to biological laws. Thus, the greatest physical similarities are found between identical twins.

The consciousness is not permanently fixed in the soma, the holo-chakra, or even in the psychosoma. It is a separate creation that resides in the mentalsoma. The shape of the psychosoma varies from one life to another, respecting and interacting with biological laws. The mentalsoma does not have a defined shape and is confined in the act of rebirth.

24. A DISTRICT IN TRANSITION

Prior to projection

Friday, September 14, 1979. Second sleep at 8:31 p.m. I laid on the right side. Temperature, 77°F. Good weather. At 7:35 p.m. I began my mental and physical detoxification and energy emission exercises, briefly losing lucidity. Due to a rather hearty dinner, unlike my usual light meals, the helpers accelerated my digestive processes in order to prepare me for this night's projection. My stomach's fullness was eliminated in a matter of minutes.

Extraphysical period

An evolved extraphysical companion sculpted the visual semblance of two extraphysical consciousnesses whom I had previously seen at some imprecise place. He commented on their conditions, explaining that I was going to visit a district in transition. I could count upon constant intangible assistance, including some probable energetic transmissions.

Within a few brief minutes, I entered an apparently peaceful garden with some extraphysical consciousnesses walking about, while others were seated or stretched out on some inviting grass. There were small, cozy environments with tables and chairs here and there among the lanes, trees, groves, stairways, verandas, short walls and living room type areas, all in a natural setting. There were no dead or dry leaves anywhere. The atmosphere was quite comfortable and bright.

My presence was noticed and three extraphysical consciousnesses immediately came by to exchange thoughts, offering friendly greetings. It was clear that, although they were communicating through "mental dialogue" (telepathy), their native language was English. They wanted to know where I came from, if I was from Earth and what I was doing and looking for at their colony. Trying to hide my projected state, I said that I came from far away and wished to know where I was.

A healthy looking youth who had appeared in the helper's visual projection, came forward and explained:

"You are in Semonta. But we want to know why you don't express yourself in our language. Where do you come from?"

The solution was to say something to avoid stirring up a long list of questions.

"I am from far away. I'm passing through. We speak Portuguese where I'm from. Where is Semonta?"

The same consciousness counter-questioned me, by this time encircled by about six others and some women with semi-lucid eyes.

"Can you help me? I have constant pain here in my head."

In view of this request, the helper's recommendation came to mind.

"Let us concentrate."

I moved away with the extraphysical consciousness and transmitted energy to him, focusing the emissions on the extraphysical brain of the suffering consciousness. I sensed the transmission of a great flow of energy that was not my own. The ailing extraphysical consciousness immediately recovered and stated:

"It's gone! I'm better!"

He went on jubilantly, leaving the group behind. The remaining extraphysical consciousnesses began to comment on the event and the situation permitted me to again ask the two closest ones the intriguing extraphysical geographical question:

"Where is Semonta?"

No one seemed to want to understand the query or explain it to me, perhaps because they were ignoring the question. Another peaceful consciousness with snow white hair, who had been meditating while reclined on one of the bordering lawns, began to exchange thoughts with me:

"I will tell you."

He walked towards one of the elevated short walls and, instantly, a map of Brazil, Paraguay, and other countries including Africa appeared forming a large section of the world map. Everything was observed by those present. At the side of the three-dimensional configurations, the extraphysical consciousness projected a ground level plan of extensive gardens and explained:

"This is Semonta. It is here, in this direction."

He drew a circle on the map, pointing to the Seychelles Islands near the African Coast, indicating the extraphysical area over the Indian Ocean. Discretely withdrawing to the place from which he had come, he slipped into his earlier sate of meditation without even waiting for my thanks.

At this point, due to the insistence of those gathering around, I had to show the area of Rio de Janeiro on the vivid map depicted on the short wall, revealing where I came from. Everyone looked surprised when other extraphysical consciousnesses arrived, and one of them, the second character whom I had seen presented in the helper's visual projection, stated firmly:

"You live on Earth and speak Portuguese. Think calmly in English, if you can, and we will be able to understand you better. We are undergoing temporary treatment here."

Accepting the suggestion, I began to slowly set forth my thoughts in English, addressing this personality by repeating what I had "heard" before at the beginning of the projection:

"You have great magnetic powers and, within a brief time, you will go back to human life. Is that right?"

The extraphysical consciousness smiled and was going to start a transmental dialogue because he recognized me, but two others brought over by the one who had had the headache, came up to invite me to a more isolated place in order to speak confidentially. It was possible to treat a few more convalescing extraphysical consciousnesses. I noticed that I was basically serving as an intermediary channel for the invisible assistance being provided from another dimension by the helpers.

I did not observe any ill consciousnesses with visible deformities or facial lesions, although there appeared to be a considerable number of mental disturbances in this small average sampling of the extraphysical population here, including repressed anxiety, concealed worries, partial amnesia, and one-track minds.

I saw no one flying. The mental imbalances of the extraphysical consciousnesses, although attenuated by the hothouses of positive energies, must have disturbed their thinking capacity, transmental comprehension and the feasibility of flight.

Upon arriving at the gardens, I immediately identified the two extraphysical consciousnesses as members of a group of consciousnesses sent to treatment centers for cleansing work, as mentioned previously.

I soon bid them farewell, as an inner transmission alerted me that it was time to return to the soma. I made it clear that, whenever possible, I avoid staying outside of the soma for more than one hour – my optimal "flight autonomy" – during my projections. I said that I would tell my human companions about the existence of the delightful extraphysical colony of Semonta where they were staying temporarily for a period of rest.

After returning

Upon awakening, I noticed a slight cramp in the left hand. The clock read 9:46 p.m. The extraphysical events came to mind firmly, little by little.

At 9:00 a.m. on Saturday morning, as I was typing the account I had written the night before, the gentleman I referred to in chapter 15, from whom a few accompanying extraphysical consciousnesses had been removed, had "coincidentally" arrived in Rio de Janeiro and telephoned to make an appointment, ignoring all that had happened during his last visit.

Observations

While projected, one experiences expanded psychic capacities, thereby facilitating the occurrence of paranormal phenomena related to projection, such as: intuition or inspiration, premonition, precognition, *déjà vu*, remote viewing, clairaudience, self-viewing, past life recall, telekinesis, telepathy, psychometry (reading of energies), bilocation, etc.

25. CONSECUTIVE PROJECTIONS

Prior to projection

Friday, September 21, 1979. Third sleep at 3:57 a.m., after writing since 2:00 a.m. in the office. Phase of the moon: new at 6:48 a.m. The night was peaceful. It was not raining. I settled into the dorsal position, noticing that the helpers were present to perform energy exercises. After some time, intense vibratory waves enveloped me and I soon fell asleep.

Extraphysical period

I awoke while flying out of the office and into the open air over Ipanema, accompanied by a youthful extraphysical male, appearing to be the equivalent of about eight (terrestrial) years old. While in rapid ascent, he mentally exalted the wonders of the sea at dawn. It was, in fact, a spectacular scene with a view of the nearby islands, a wisp of clouds in the distance, and the ocean stretching out as far as I could see. It was interesting to note that the perspective of the scenery appeared totally modified when viewing it from higher up. The Atlantic Ocean seemed to have expanded and become filled with lights. My range of vision became greatly enlarged, and the immense seascape spread out beautifully before me.

The dark-complexioned boy, whose serene eyes conveyed radiant goodwill, began to comment on the natural healing energies that the sea offers sick intraphysical and extraphysical consciousnesses. He suggested that I enhance my extraphysical vision through my will-power in order to see with greater clarity. The vastness of the sea water, of the sky and the spiral clouds actually expanded the horizon's boundaries, providing a broader view than if I had been aboard a jumbo jet.

I thought I would have many facts to describe, in view of my encounter with this child who had as much knowledge as an extraphysical adult. But an indefinable discomfort called my psychosoma to return to the soma.

After returning

Upon arriving in my bedroom, abruptly entering the soma and immediately awakening, I heard the unmistakable noise inside my head, characteristic of the sudden realignment of the bodies. This forceful sound, which I have heard so many times in repeated experiences, is difficult to translate into words and varies slightly each time.

It seemed as though a can full of dried beans had been suddenly poured over an aluminum container – making a very sudden noise that sounded like "cheerroh" inside my head. The sound had a sonorous quality with the "rroh" part being strong and short.

When I regained lucidity, I could still feel the up-and-down motion of the spring mattress, appearing to coincide with the spontaneous movement of my wife, who was laying at my side. The vibrations resulting from her movement had reached my soma, causing me to be deeply startled, and had been the cause of the urgent pull on the silver cord. Was the rapid arrival of the psychosoma perhaps due to the fact that I had been projected only a few yards from the apartment in a light altered state of consciousness at the time?

The memories of the boy and the sea suddenly came back to me. Moving the still numb soma out of the dorsal position, I checked the clock. It read 5:02 in the morning. Upon turning onto the left side, I continued to detect the presence of the child. That is why I tried a second takeoff.

Extraphysical period

In a few moments I rejoined the boy, this time in the office of my apartment in a follow-up projection. He had brought along a middle-aged extraphysical male who looked familiar to me, yet I did not recall his name or where he was from.

The extraphysical consciousness, although tranquil, was not fully aware of the surroundings. I attended him while he sat in my office facing the Atlantic Ocean. The boy insisted on seeing if I would remember the sick male while I was free from the restrictions of the physical brain. My recollection of his identity would then facilitate the transmission of energy to him due to the profound affinity between the two of us. After a few moments, I was able to recall the man's identity. I had met him a few times about three decades earlier when he was a young student, perhaps in 1949. He had been among those attending the cleansing sessions in the Uberabense Spiritist Center in Minas Gerais state, then directed by Major Nestor Cravo.

I did not recall his name. Deep within me, however, I perceived his identity, and was convinced that it was indeed him, now more mature and in the condition of an extraphysical consciousness.

The boy then brought another man, perhaps more than seventy years old and apparently paralytic, who showed senility in his non-stop speech. The lad indicated with great satisfaction that the sick man had been his grandfather in his latest intraphysical period. The pleasant, well dressed man, with a stiff white mustache, thin white hair, a small head and short body, expressed enormous enthusiasm over the presence of his grandson, who was devotedly caring for him. The way he dealt with the sick men indicated that he would be a doctor in his next intraphysical life.

My intuition revealed that the boy was a ward of Ascensão, an extraphysical colony located in the area over the state of Minas Gerais. This is the same colony where Tancredo, the boy referred to in chapter 3, had been staying.

After the youth attended the sick men for a few more minutes, I bid them farewell, returned to the bedroom and experienced a routine re-alignment of the bodies.

After returning

The clock read 5:31 in the morning. I had no time to write down this account, as it was almost time for me to get out of bed and go to work. My wife, after waking, listened patiently, as always, to my description of the two consecutive projections. The act of narrating helped me to retain the details of the events.

26. INVESTMENT SUGGESTIONS

Prior to projection

Sunday, September 23, 1979. Room temperature: 71.6°F. I went to bed at 6:57 p.m. in the dorsal position. After a few minutes, I turned onto the left side.

Extraphysical period

I became fully awake inside an ample building in a district of a European metropolis. I was accompanied by an extraphysical consciousness who requested that I remain calm and be observant of the local surroundings.

We passed through some well furnished, but empty, reception areas and offices. In an outlying room, we saw an elegant and very respectable looking elderly man, who was busy with some documents at the door of an immense safe.

In the next room on the left, a man in his forties sat alone on a couch apparently in intense concentration, with his eyes closed and his arms resting on the back of the couch. Two other rooms to the right were occupied: one by a mature looking extraphysical male and the other by two persons, all quite relaxed in chairs, seated in front of desks, and completely absorbed by their own activities.

Now having an overall view of the luxuriously furnished offices, and still accompanied by an alert and tranquil extraphysical consciousness, I identified the thoughts coming from the minds of the concentrating gentlemen. I was shocked and was able to control myself only due to other surprises I have handled in the past. I quickly understood the nature and extent of the activities occurring in complete silence and without any assistants or support staff on this night shift between Sunday and Monday. These men were transmitting intense mental suggestions to certain other persons utilizing thought at a distance!

The scenes in the psychospheres (auras) of the isolated men were unmistakable. One of them was concentrating so hard that his whole face was wrinkled up. As he did so, the purpose of their routine mental efforts became clear. They were trying to influence

businessmen to make major investment decisions, probably during the next day.

Astonished upon discovering the purpose of this telepathically transmitted hypnosis, I wanted to get a little closer to the man on my right, to the front of the couch where he was seated. A large photo of an unfamiliar gray-haired gentleman stood out from the numerous documents spread out on the desk. This was the victim. I was surprised to see the image of the potential client come to the surface of this long-distance suggestion technique that was more sophisticated and dishonest than I ever imagined could exist. This was a war of thoughts, with unimaginable repercussions in both worlds. It was "contemporary voodoo" in the hunt for money with subtle, inferior purposes and devoid of any good intentions.

I was informed that this was psychic exploitation at its worst because its power was used against those who were unwary or mentally unprotected – typically the heads of enterprises or companies upon which thousands of people depended for their physical survival.

Still stunned by the sight of the papers, the photo and the ideas, and not wishing to accept the reality of these mental insertions, I went to view the two other rooms. Unfortunately, the same thing was going on there. The only difference was that the two "white collar" workers in the thought control chamber were concentrating together, calmly weaving mental currents with no break in rhythm, vigorously trying to modify the mental attitude of a single victim.

The extraphysical consciousness at my side mentally followed my observations on the extent of human debauchery, where the most sublime resources of the energy of thoughts, capable of yielding cures and everlasting happiness, are subverted for the purpose of influencing businessmen in order to increase personal wealth, which is inevitably lost upon the death of the soma.

It was explained to me that the atmosphere of these offices was a little heavier and more difficult than that of the ordinary business space due to invasion by capricious, sick extraphysical consciousnesses, who were very good at playing dishonest mental games, and who "assisted" the hypnotists to manipulate those under remote hypnosis. These cohorts had been temporarily removed to allow us to peacefully and carefully examine the surroundings. The extraphysical consciousness commented:

"In answer to insistent queries, we see here the natural obstacle to the widespread development of the phenomenon of projection. Can you imagine the projector who nourishes such intentions? The negative suggestions could have much more disastrous effects when applied directly. Nevertheless, the *cosmo-ethic* cannot be fooled. The inevitable consequences may appear to be slow in arriving, but they always come. No one is exempt from being the victim of their own negative works."

Could Mesmer, Charcot and other luminaries in the history of hypnotism have ever imagined an operation like this, so highly systematized, on such solid but decadent foundations? The secret and methodical character of the activities in this environment was a fact, and the seriousness of the enterprise unfortunately left no room for doubt.

Lawlessness is being practiced and it is going unnoticed. Worst of all, it is going unpunished because it is not within the reach of human laws whose penal and civil codes still do not have provisions prohibiting infractions of this kind. Police organizations still have not awakened to this reality, being too burdened by common assaults to consider the improper use of the most powerful weapon available to criminals: misdirected thosenes which affect those open to that type of influence.

It is worth asking: What is the limit of the powers of the mind? What are the ultimate means that can be used in the struggle for personal interests? If carefully thought out decisions can be influenced by certain persons, what can be said of the effect that extraphysical consciousnesses can have on people's hasty decisions?

I did not accompany the events as they progressed through the night and into the morning. Nevertheless, who can tell whether any of these men, so dedicated to the trade of transmitting suggestions over a distance would not, from their office or home, leave the soma in the middle of the night and directly persuade the unwary?

It is possible for sick intraphysical and extraphysical consciousnesses with bad intentions to consciously or unconsciously provoke considerable mental damage to those who have not cultivated mental discipline. This fact raises a myriad of political and social issues which, sooner or later, must be seriously considered by human organizations. It is for this reason that projection constitutes the most transcendent psychic manifestation, as it involves many sectors of intraphysical life.

After observing that "princely den of thieves" for some time, I left the exquisitely furnished locale in a thoughtful, slow return to my physical base, in the company of the helper.

After returning

Upon awakening, the soma was still laying on the left side. Within seconds, the events of the projection came to me in their entirety. Still shocked by what I had witnessed, I felt an invisible affirmation that I should register the projection without delay in order to illustrate extraphysical reality. I did so after verifying the time: 8:44 p.m. It was not possible to determine the time that had been spent in the environment I visited, but it had certainly taken place during the night.

Observations

This night's excursion reminded me of news about the interest of powerful governments in the use of projection as a means of spying on other nations, including the temporary appropriation, copying, and subsequent return of secret strategic defense plans. I think that this is possible in the crustal dimension (coexisting extraphysical duplicate of the physical dimension). However, the question of transporting objects with consecutive dematerialization and re-materialization is extremely problematic when non-cosmoethical objectives come into play.

I would never submit to such experiments in view of their purpose, as they constitute a nasty business for the experimenter. The preservation of the noble aspect of projection is fundamental to maintaining the projector's consciential balance and the quality of his or her extraphysical companions.

27. THE PSYCHOLOGIST'S PATIENT

Prior to projection

Tuesday, September 25, 1979. Room temperature: 71.6°F with the use of the air conditioner, as it was up to 95.9°F outside, being the first hot day after a period of cooler weather. One air conditioner was left running in the office, with the door facing the hallway open to the bedroom, thus attenuating the characteristic monotonous sound. I was called by the helpers to go to bed, around 9:57 p.m.

Using vigorous energy exercises, the helpers gathered, chased away, and assisted other extraphysical consciousnesses for about a half-an-hour. I noticed that some energies were even transmitted to my wife Elisabeth who slept on the right side of the bed. I went to sleep in the dorsal position.

Extraphysical period

Having successfully projected from the soma, I noticed a cleansing being performed with some inferior extraphysical consciousnesses wearing grim expressions. They were being retained by the helpers in the extraphysical environment of the physical base (my bedroom) where they hurled a continuous stream of blasphemies.

After a few moments of preliminary activities beside a sinister-looking pair of extraphysical consciousnesses, the energetic density of the situation forced my "strategic retreat." I quickly returned to the soma. I appeared to be a prisoner of a powerful net of energy.

The sudden intentional return to the soma from above, allowed me to once again hear the peculiar sound of an intracranial noise (see glossary), typical of the violent reintegration of the psychosoma with the soma. On this occasion, it sounded like the short, fast crack of a whip. The clock read 10:54 p.m. I turned the soma onto the left side and, having replenished my strength, proceeded to take off again.

The separation of the psychosoma occurred instantly. The dark, fearsome extraphysical consciousnesses were waiting for my return into the improvised arena, anxious for continued energetic confrontations.

After a while, the atmosphere became a little more serene when some psychotic post-mortems were taken away for recovery. It was now time to return to the soma again in order to replenish my energies and continue working.

My return to the soma and peaceful awakening, allowed me to recall some of the extraphysical events. The clock read 11:56 p.m. After a few minutes of mental and emotional revitalization, I lay on the stomach and left side of the face and began a new projection. I fearlessly went forward to finish the work at hand.

The most pathological extraphysical consciousness of the group was awaiting my separation from the soma in order to engage in a direct dialogue.

The completely unbalanced consciousness had the appearance of a 4-foot-tall woman dressed in a plain, wrinkled, blue outfit. Her facial features reminded me of a parrot with uncontrolled bloodshot eyes in their orbits, shimmering with indescribable anguish and the mentality of a spoiled eight-year-old child. She was unable to entirely control her movements.

It was necessary to hold her with my hands, and embrace her as if she were a child. With the assistance of the helpers, who I could not see at the time, I tried to use a deep suggestion for her to sleep. After a while of serving as nanny and nurse, with spontaneous fraternal compassion inspired by the sick one, it was possible to induce her to sleep with her cadaver-like eyes still open. Then came the suggestion that I stand up and hold that consciousness for some time until her extraphysical sleep took hold.

In a short while, one of the helpers took the sick one away.

A few of the extraphysical antagonists tried to subvert the restraining vibratory system, but something suddenly happened that scared them, forcing their immediate departure. I then experienced a peaceful return to the soma. My night's task was over, creating an intense, internal peace. Extraphysical assistance in the form of cleansing projections is extremely gratifying.

After returning

Upon awakening, the clear, vibrant recollection of the sick woman's sad features, particularly the eyes, remained in my mind. I checked the time: 12:58 a.m. After this third consecutive projection, the helpers explained the extraphysical situation that had just transpired.

The unhappy extraphysical consciousnesses had been attracted by my wife Elisabeth, who had been used as "extraphysical bait" in order to help the mother of one of our son Arthur's friends. According to Elisabeth, the little girl was under psychological treatment, at the recommendation of the school authorities. Everything now became clear. The woman's sick extraphysical company had been coupled to the hyperactive child. After exchanging ideas with Elisabeth about the occurrences, I started to write them down. As I was registering this projection, I reaffirmed that all human gratification is insignificant in comparison with the benevolence of the helpers.

28. OPPORTUNE ADVICE

Prior to projection

Friday, September 28, 1979. Third sleep. I laid down on the right side at 2:22 a.m. after brief energy exercises. The apparatus hanging on the bedroom wall indicated the temperature to be 75°F, with variable weather and 75% humidity. This data is provided in consideration of those who wish to study the relationship between the atmosphere of the physical base and projective takeoff.

Extraphysical period

I became lucid in the extraphysical dimension among several extraphysical consciousnesses who informed me that I would visit a distant extraphysical region. And it really was! After going through several different locales and ambiances, I reached the entrance of a colony where sick extraphysical consciousnesses are treated.

After a while, a happy, energetic extraphysical consciousness full of vitality suddenly appeared in the area. I recognized him immediately as José Pedro de Freitas – the famous and unforgettable medium "Arigó"[1].

I was thrilled to see him! When I recovered from the very pleasant surprise, I was going to tell him of the latest news such as the phone call from his brother Eli a few weeks ago, a documentary about his life that is being shown in the United States, and dozens of other subjects, when he quickly cut me off in his characteristic way:

"No! Let's not talk about those things! I don't feel good talking about me. Intraphysical life is a little complicated. I want to talk about you. So, you are part of the "pajama squad" that goes around with okra in the psychosoma! Come on, tell me about it!"

---

[1]José Arigó – Famous Brazilian medium who channeled the extraphysical consciousness Dr. Fritz. Both became celebrities, performing surgical operations using only a scalpel or a simple knife that was rarely cleaned and sometimes showed signs of rust. Following are three common characteristics of psychic surgery: 1. Little or no bleeding; 2. No anesthesia; 3. No antisepsis.

I tried to show him that I was an apprentice to the helpers in those services which require dedication and willingness to perform correctly, but he interrupted my elaborate mental dissertation saying:

"Waldo, you know I was told around here that you went flying around like a crazy man with your son, among other things. Let me give you some advice. Take this work seriously. Projections and physical effects are at the root of everything. I had many projections in my life, but there wasn't enough time to connect everything together. My life was very distressed. Don't be that way. Take it seriously. That is how we are able to learn more."

Then, another extraphysical consciousness came in to talk with him. I observed that he listened with patience and understanding. Appearing younger and thinner, Arigó exhibited great intelligence. He was not a patient at the colony, but an active extraphysical medical assistant. He hardly resembled the Arigó who had died in an automobile accident years before.

After retaking control of the conversation and making attempts to receive and retain the observations made by Arigó, he appeared to want to conclude the interview, fraternally lamenting:

"Well, I really wanted to fly with you to a beautiful place that I know but, as you know, I can't. I'm on duty."

We said good-bye. I am grateful to Arigó and the helpers who made this unforgettable meeting of great significance and opportune warning possible. It has provoked much meditation and analysis of facts regarding errors of omission and the maximization of benefits to be derived from intraphysical existence and the exchange allowed by projection.

After returning

Right after awakening, the recall of this night's serious and surprising projection came to me, strangely enough, without the signal of the energetic cord's "summons." The clock showed 4:13 a.m. In the bedroom, I could only hear the sound of the air conditioner coming from the office.

29. AN EXTRAPHYSICAL PUBLIC EVENT

Prior to projection

Saturday, September 29, 1979. I went to bed at 8:23 p.m., laying on the left side. Ambient temperature: 77°F. Variable weather, with a relative humidity of 59%.

Extraphysical period

I awoke before entering a sinister-looking city, accompanying an extraphysical consciousness who was going to someone's aid. I was visiting in the role of an observer under the guise of an extraphysical consciousness. My psychosoma was denser, due to the low energetic pattern in this locale. I was wearing a bizarre garment, and the silver cord had been disguised in order to hide my status as a projector.

Upon receiving a briefing on this projection, I realized that it was not the first time I had done this. I recalled previous similar excursions, including one which had occurred while living in Uberaba, almost twenty years before.

The tense, shadowy surroundings, reminded me of scenes in certain comic book horror stories. One could see that many artists must have been inspired by similar cities in order to compose settings, characters and plots.

I could see preparations being made for a medieval, public, religious ritual where there were sick extraphysical consciousnesses. They had dense, human-like psychosomas with terrible deformities, aberrations and imbalances resulting in the total distortion of the psychosoma. All those present were "piled up" in unspeakable promiscuity.

In order to enter the grounds through one of the immense, arched doorways reminiscent of ancient cities, those unable to fly, being in the majority, were being forced to march through a narrow pass in rows of two between a company of guards who were screening the visitors at the gate.

Under the arches, I looked attentively at the inscriptions, sculptures and carvings of dubious taste on the main gate, which reminded me of an imitation of the Arch of Triumph in Paris.

Each extraphysical consciousness had to identify himself by revealing his status and indicating the ideology he was affiliated with by pointing to one of the encrusted insignias. Some passed through, while others were taken aside by the huge guards, who were armed with spears to control the herd of humanoid beasts. The distressing spectacle inspired compassion for some and unbearable repulsion towards others.

I paid customary homage to one of the huge guards whose shield bore a masculine effigy with an eagle-like nose and long face which, from a distance, suggested the profile of an English noble. I then received permission to pass and descend along the cliff toward the public square where the night's activities were going to be held.

Upon crossing the square, I witnessed the epileptic-like seizures of some of the sick ones stretched out on the ground who had come to be cured by the local healers in their group hypnosis.

The preparations in the square struck me as being parody of the manifestations I had witnessed in July of 1953 in Buenos Aires during an event honoring the memory of Evita Peron, where large groups of sick people were brought on stretchers to pray and to receive healings from the holy woman. On that occasion, there were many sick people with Parkinson's disease in the flower beds, with a gigantic picture several stories tall, of their political-religious patron saint, there in the middle of *Avenida de Maio*.

Crossing the square that would be used for the public celebrations, I could see chairs, stalls and long benches already half-filled by those arriving. We looked for the crude house where an extraphysical consciousness anonymously performing work of renunciation and self-denial was temporarily living. It is strange to speak of *anonymous work of renunciation*, but that was the reality of the situation.

I do not have adequate words to describe the atmosphere of that *sinister city*. In the desolate and parched setting, one could see no ornamental trees or public water fountains; only dark swampy water. There was no pleasant light anywhere. An inescapable layer of smoke filled the suffocating extraphysical surroundings.

From time to time, one could see the confusion caused by a group breaking out in a tumult, causing the unfortunate consciousnesses with transfigured faces to run in all directions. The implacable vigilantes would always be found in the middle of the confusion. In these explosions of scorn, intemperance and revolt, the most horrible expressions were shouted by the deformed extraphysical consciousnesses, sometimes appearing to be engaged in playful camaraderie. It was possible to hear decades-old Portuguese swear words that had fallen out of use in Brazil.

I got the impression that this extraphysical citadel was not too far from Rio de Janeiro. Those present were speaking Portuguese using old slang and expressions, and used outdated mannerisms. The majority of this population were not even able to express themselves telepathically – a capacity that is so natural for the consciousness liberated from physical form. They were apparently only able to communicate by articulating words "vocally" as though they were still human.

The extraphysical consciousnesses in attendance lived with various other suffering consciousnesses in an area that, according to the helper who was beside me, was one of the cleanest around. Even so, it was in an indescribable state of camouflaged filth, exuding a nauseating mustiness which would disgust any average visitor.

Moments before arriving at the square where everyone was supposed to be, three squads of guards came checking inside the poor, rundown shack which finally emptied as all the residents left to participate in the public event. The soldiers were hopelessly trying to impose silence in the pandemonium there as more people arrived. At this point, three pygmies, who must have been the secret agents of the authorities, appeared brandishing swords and proceeded directly with the formal questioning of all those present in the area. In moments, they were headed in my direction. I instantly sensed that I had been discovered as a clandestine projector. To escape, I resorted to a drastic recourse I was shown during the briefing before the excursion. I had to steady my thoughts and fly with all possible energy far away from the environment. I did so and the pygmies were soon below me, looking up and indignantly shaking their swords at me in the gray air. I do not know why, but I felt as though the swords could have done me harm. In what way? I had had the same feeling when I saw the guards' spears.

My upward departure from the locale was not easy. The flight was most difficult. The helper stayed behind to carry out the remainder of the initiated task while I returned much faster than I had come. In a few instants, I was being attracted towards the soma. It was like finding a life preserver during a critical emergency. It was worse than a nightmare, because I had been entirely lucid.

After returning

I immediately awoke and, as I saw the time, 9:54 p.m., the memories came to me calmly in their entirety. Perhaps no projector can avoid remembering such an experience. The energy transmission from a helper signaled me to register the projection. It gave me the impression of emitting life-giving energy in all directions. It had the effect of cleaning the environment from the energetic remnants of the viscous, harmful forces that insisted on remaining in the room.

Observations

A few words about extraphysical flight. The brain of the psychosoma has neural circuits with kinetic memory, or memory of motion. These memory banks organize, program and execute extraphysical flight. Not only the preparation for takeoff but also the types of flight, such as high altitude, long range and rapid free flight.

Lucid projectors often disguise their projected state in order not to embarrass others and to be able to perform tasks. They can be noticed due to the luminescence of the psychosoma, the act of flight and their appearance. Projectors can also hide their silver cord.

It is common for the projected visitor to "switch off" the radiant light of the psychosoma while in shadowy districts in order to appear to be in the same condition as the extraphysical inhabitants.

The act of avoiding flight where there are extraphysical consciousnesses who are incapable of flying is another attitude taken by those aware of multidimensional reality. Assuming an opaque and a less pleasant extraphysical appearance when in an ambiance of an inferior nature, permits greater liberty and anonymity to the extraphysical consciousness when in extraphysical regions where this is warranted. Projectors can use the three resources mentioned above, as well as a masking of the silver cord, in order to appear to be an extraphysical consciousness, when extraphysical circumstances require.

No one comes to the intraphysical dimension solely for pleasure, and the same is true of projections. The extraphysical world of the projector presents impressive extremes of astounding beauty and horrid ugliness, attractive and repulsive aspects, sentiments of hope and moments of tension.

In conclusion, there are many people living in better conditions as humans than they would, and perhaps will, as extraphysical consciousnesses. How many and which of us? How incredibly right were Dante and Swedenbörg! The projection of the psychosoma represents a preparation for, or a dry run of, biological death and the upcoming multidimensional experience.

30. THE SHAPE OF A GHOST

Prior to projection

Thursday, October 4, 1979. Third sleep at 2:11 a.m. Ambient temperature: 73°F. I had turned off the air conditioner sometime before. I laid down on the right side.

I remained completely lucid while in alignment with the soma. The soma was lying on its right side on the left edge of the bed.

Extraphysical period

A pale yellowish light appeared that illuminated everything as if immense eyelids had suddenly opened over a pair of inner eyes deep within me. I clearly perceived only the upper part of my body, or rather, the extraphysical head, arms and hands along with my extended extraphysical feet, all together at the edge of the bed. The rest of the psychosoma had not manifested.

I was impressed by the sensation of being a bodiless creation of smoke filled with will and thoughts, like an immense intelligent amoebae in a science-fiction story, and with more life and reasoning capacity than a soma of flesh and blood. Images came to mind of an anchored ship, planes tied down against strong winds, and of semi-materialized extraphysical consciousnesses during materialization sessions using ectoplasm (dense, semi-physical energy).

Upon clapping my white extraphysical hands, I noticed that they looked as though they were under gentle sunlight. With the form of the psychosoma partially composed, I felt the surface of the golden-yellow carpet of my bedroom. Upon brushing the carpet with the palms of my extraphysical hands in order to inspect it, I recalled the floor beneath it and, at the same moment, was able to observe the wooden tiles of the floor. After rubbing my hands on the wooden tiles, I saw a light emanating from everywhere illuminating the pieces of wood that were joined to each other.

I thought of further inspecting the physical installations of the room, when an indefinable discomfort arose within me. I realized that I was too close to the dense body. I was still within the range of the more powerful influence of the silver cord – a condition that occurs when one is up to thirteen feet from the soma. The psychosoma was on the floor, only partially formed. With the admonitory discomfort being so strong, it was better to return to the soma.

All these thoughts transpired in only tenths of a second. I awoke immediately without any lapse in lucidity. I think that, when operating from the psychosoma while it is still in alignment with the soma, the mental processes of the extraphysical brain of the psychosoma give the impression of occurring at lightning speed.

The partial formation of the psychosoma next to the soma was due to the quick takeoff of the psychosoma and the minimal emission of consciential energy. Where is the sensation of discomfort situated within this living fog?

The appearance of the psychosoma is dependent upon the mental state of the projector. Illnesses and disturbances of the soma and the mind generally alter the psychosoma for the worse. A good state of health and extraphysical lucidity rejuvenate, harmonize and improve the form of the psychosoma.

I did not notice any extraphysical consciousnesses in the vicinity.

After returning

I consulted the clock. It was 2:38 a.m. I was indecisive as to whether or not I would get up right away to make this entry. I chose to get up and, after a few seconds, upon arriving at the corridor close to my study, the bodies still seemed to be fairly out of alignment (partially projected). This gave the sensation of walking in emptiness. I had to stop where I was, increase my lucidity to waking state level by willfully emitting waves of energy in order to enable myself to go through the doorway of my study.

Every time this occurs, I have the sensation that I am wasting a seething force that emanates from the soma. It might be better to immediately begin another projection, but I always worry about forgetting the extraphysical events that have just transpired. It is a fact that I almost always forget some part of a projection. For this reason, the solution has been to write the account in the moment and continue with another projection later, when possible.

Upon trying to sleep again, at 3:31 a.m., my wife, at my side, was snoring rather loudly. Not wanting to wake her, I thought it best to go to the living room, taking two pillows with me.

I closed the curtains and the window, stopped the noisy pendulum of the clock at 4:14 a.m. and laid on the right side over three modules of a sectional couch. My head pointed towards geographical north in this new environment. Two roosters crowed simultaneously in the dawn of Ipanema.

Extraphysical period

In a few moments, I was once again lucid and outside the body, floating above the couch modules in the middle of the living room.

It occurred to me to view my sleeping dense body. Upon attentively examining my tranquil, left facial profile, noting the closed eyes, a feeling of pity and gratitude arose in me for the apparatus before me. It seemed as though it belonged to someone else. It had permitted me so many experiences throughout my life. I now understood all the more how the soma is a useful instrument.

It is always touching to see the inert soma as if the psychosoma were a mirror image, contemplating it with its emptied brain. At these times, it is the reflected image's turn to act on its own. This is the greatest triumph of mind over matter, the crucial experiment of being human. The contemplation of the defenseless soma sharpened my objective of observing and learning. Seeing one's own incapacitated soma is a doorway to self-knowledge. It is the first step towards one's inner self.

Meditating on the enormity of my debt to this extraordinary vehicle, I found myself arriving at the conclusion: "One day I will see it for the last time."

Watching a movie or looking at a picture is quite different from observing your own dense body. The soma is the straightjacket of the consciousness, the prison of flesh and blood while in the intraphysical dimension. It is wrapped around you like a miserable corpse, an empty shell, a turned-off machine or something of the like. Which is the duplicate of which, the soma or the psychosoma? Am I living *and* "dead"? That is a new twist on Shakespeare's "To be or not to be."

After a few moments of calm reflection devoid of narcissism, a sentiment of gratitude for the machine-prison that has let me consciously take leave of it so many times gave me the desire to touch the motionless face with the fingers of the right extra-physical hand in order to embrace myself.

I touched the tips of my extraphysical fingers to my physical face and automatically slipped, with incredible rapidity, into the soma, completely returning through the side of the dense body. This is a repercussion which is difficult to avoid when one is projected very close to the soma, because of the intimacy and strength of the connection of the silver cord while at close proximity.

After returning

Upon awakening, I had thoughts of gratitude for the soma. I remembered the impossibility of telling the time, as the digital clock was in the bedroom. After a while, having lost all sleepiness, and having completely awakened after two consecutive projections, I returned the pillows to the bedroom and noted the time to be 4:54 a.m. The hygrometer showed 68%. I began to register this second small self-induced projection which had taken place in the living room.

Observations

The brain, the most complex of cellular organs, only stops functioning upon the impact of biological death. It has two fundamental and distinct states of operation. The human soma functions with the consciousness present in the waking state, during dreams, in ordinary sleep, as well as in other altered states of consciousness. It functions without the presence of the consciousness during a projection.

There are two cases of "empty brain." The consciousness can be projected outside the physical brain during a projection of the mentalsoma, in which case the psychosoma remains in alignment with the soma. The consciousness can also be projected outside the body in the psychosoma, in which case the mentalsoma and psychosoma will be in alignment.

These states wherein the consciousness is outside the brain, or the "empty brain" condition, will call profound attention to medical researchers in decades to come. The comprehension of the workings of the coronal-chakra(crown chakra), the energetic cord and the mentalsoma are the keys to understanding the "empty brain" condition.

31.   RECURRENT PROJECTION

Prior to takeoff

Wednesday, October 10, 1979. Third sleep. I laid down on the right side at 3:55 a.m., after writing in the study for about an hour-and--a-half. Temperature: 79°F. Barometric readings indicated meteorological instability. Humidity: 72%.

Extraphysical period

I slowly achieved lucidity in front of the covered electric typewriter sitting on the table in the study where I had been writing by hand minutes before. How had I gotten here? I was alone. It seemed as if this projection had resulted from an unconscious act or mechanical movement promoted by a series of actions performed during the waking state prior to the projective state – a case of automatic behavior. Before going to sleep I had told myself that I would type in the morning what I had handwritten earlier at dawn, as I sometimes do. The subconscious mind suggested the action and the suggestion was acted upon. I have observed that the consciousness can have spontaneous projections even when not undergoing shock, accident or illness.

As I contemplated the typewriter and sensed that I was able to see inside of it, as though the instrument were made of crystal, a satisfying thought came to me.

"I am projected. Here I go!"

Feeling at peace with life and thinking with great ease, I realized that I had actually been waiting for this occasion, having been feeding this location to my subconscious as a projective target. I was certain that I was not dreaming due to the liveliness, lucidity and peculiar charm of the projection. The psychosoma, being dense enough to be exteriorized intact, appeared to be filled with energy. Flying quite rapidly out through the study window towards the Atlantic Ocean, this willful catapulting had thrown me forward in a headlong rush of thoughts.

In a very short time I arrived at the interior of a long hall in a deserted temple. I was aware of having been there before. I also recalled the extraphysical consciousnesses who had been present at this site a year earlier, receiving extraphysical assistance from the helpers. As I passed through the interior of the temple, I noticed that the front of the construction had neither windows nor doors. The hall, located on the second floor, had a large entrance on the left side and another at the back. I had arrived through the entrance next to the right-hand corner.

An old wish returned to me to read the inscriptions inscribed on the stones and ceramic pieces, but I was unable to do so. The walls were thick. The ceiling was about 16 feet high, and the room was about 30 feet long and 50 feet wide. The interior of the closed temple was clean and in good condition. There was no vegetation growing on the inside walls. The air was still. There were signs of humidity next to one of the staircases.

I saw a painted figure of a black man with open arms and legs on one of the rocks. No extraphysical consciousnesses were discernible in the interior of the completely silent temple which was clearly illuminated with an orange light.

I was convinced that I was in Africa, in a dense jungle area previously unexplored by modern man. This visit was one in a series that I had made to that place over a period of time. This, then, was a typical case of a recurrent projection, or one that is repeated because a consciousness likes the location and develops a series of experiments with the intention of studying the details of the locale, exploring its history and collecting data related to that district. Why? Simple whim, an emotional link or magnetic attraction to the place ?

I continued to contemplate the inscribed ceramics on this floor, feeling the gravitating energies of this environment, when the body's energetic call came and I re-entered the body from the side moments later, to my great disappointment.

After returning

I awoke to find the soma lying on its right side. I did not know how long the projection had lasted. The clock showed 4:36 a.m. Roosters crowed announcing the new day and I awakened without suffering any lapse of lucidity. The brain was engaged in gathering the most minute memories of the flight. The joy resulting from this conscious projection persisted throughout the day.

32. PROJECTIONS WITH WITNESSES

Prior to projection

Sunday, October 14, 1979. I went to bed at 8:25 p.m. Temperature: 75° F. Humidity: 62%. I laid down in the dorsal position, with feet apart and hands over the legs. Intensive energy emission exercises began through contractions of the chewing muscles and typical movements with the arms and hands, under the guidance of the extraphysical consciousness, José Grosso. After a few minutes, another helper, not identified, resolutely transmitted the idea to me that as soon as I felt a hand on my forehead, as had already occurred on past occasions, I should try to keep my thoughts still and concentrate on the act of projecting. The helpers would then try to facilitate my totally lucid takeoff. After perhaps about 40 minutes, during which I maintained concentration and the decided will to project myself, an invisible right hand appeared resting on the center of my forehead, pressing the area between the eyebrows with the palm. I felt the energetic manifestations of the frontal-chakra.

I felt the vibrational state become stronger. I made a mental attempt at taking off, without using any physical exertion. The soma remained rigid regardless. I took off in a classic upward departure, leaving my inanimate soma covered only by a thin white bedspread. I floated up to a distance of more-or-less thirteen feet above the soma on the bed.

Extraphysical period

As I assumed a vertical position, the suggestion came to me to lay the psychosoma in the dorsal position once again. This occurred several times as if I were taking a repeated takeoff training test

At one point in that extraphysical "lie-down/stand-up" exercise, I looked for a better position above the soma, and moved in order to be at right angles to the bed. On another occasion, I stayed in the opposite position with the head of the psychosoma beside the physical feet. During one of the departures, I felt the transition state of double consciousness, seeming to be partly in the soma and partly in the psychosoma, having some lucidity in both conditions simultaneously, predominating first in one place and then in the other, according to the location of mental focus. In fact, the consciousness never divides itself. However, one's perception seems to be double, or in two places at once.

On the first takeoff, I experienced a brief moment of perfectly bearable discomfort, due to the powerful vibrations of the process. In subsequent instances, no other unpleasant state occurred. Quite to the contrary, the event brought me an intense sense of satisfaction, seeming like an inner expansion and a deep sense of well-being.

I now wished to see my target person. I wanted to see my wife, who was watching a television program in the living room. But the projector does not always succeed in going where he or she wishes. It was possible for me to raise the psychosoma over the bed three times, enjoy the sensation of being literally out of the body, and reach the corridor and the door of the living room. Then the powerful silver cord called the psychosoma back, as if its energy level was low. The silver cord behaved as though it were made of rubber, alternately stretching and returning to its original form.

This fact demonstrated that the psychosoma remained within the area of the silver cord's vigorous influence for the duration of the projection. Evidently, I was working on neutralizing the energetic cord's sensitivity.

The intervals between the departures from and the smooth re-entries into the soma allowed me to feel like never before, with exacting detail, the partial separations of the extraphysical legs and extraphysical arms that seemed to float as if they were pieces of light cloth, similar to fine silk, that occasionally received a gust of wind, being blown from side to side. The comparison of the psychosoma to small air balloons of light, fine material is quite close to the sensation that one experiences during projection.

The first takeoff seems so simple and easy, but upon re-entering the soma, the situation becomes complex and it becomes more difficult to leave the soma each time thereafter.

For the first time, the feeling came to me of being observed by a "cloud of witnesses" that piled up around me, in the extended bedroom. It was as if it were a wide anatomy amphitheater, where the "guinea pig" was being examined by dozens of extraphysical consciousnesses the way that students follow surgery classes through observation windows. This was confirmed later by helpers when they explained that the extraphysical consciousnesses were united in research and study, striving for the future development of their personal projective capacity. They were observing my experimental departures and returns to the body, paying attention to the details of the process. This is why my extraphysical liberty had been restricted by the silver cord, that consistently pulled the psychosoma back to the physical base.

This confirms the news about the intentions of the more developed extraphysical consciousnesses of intensifying the practice of lucid projection throughout this planet.

The soma resembled the long bark of a tree trunk that merely filled up when the psychosoma re-entered it. Who can express that sensation fully? One can ask: fill the dense, compact, massive, continuous and organ-filled body with what? Nevertheless, it fills all of it, molecule by molecule, cell by cell, millimeter by millimeter, in a complete coexistence and interdependence .

In my first projection to the door of the living room, my visual capacity improved. The orange extraphysical brightness of the ambiance, which was physically dark, intensified from an extraphysical point of view. Every time I went through the closed bedroom door leading to the corridor, both the bedroom and the corridor seemed to be much larger than they actually were.

Next to the left wall of the corridor, which was usually empty, I saw an extraphysical object about 32" high and 28" wide that looked like a piece of cloth-covered furniture. Could it have been an extraphysical accessory?

The third time I was projected in the corridor, after repeatedly going back to the soma and returning again – as if practicing stretching the silver cord – I saw a calm extraphysical consciousness about to enter the bedroom of my young son Arthur, who was sleeping. I was going to approach it, when the soma called me irresistibly to return. This time, it was not possible for me to leave the soma again.

I returned to the soma from above. This imposed return occurred because, while relaxing in the dorsal position, my mouth had stayed open, causing me to snore. The noise that was produced had interrupted the projection.

I tried still another takeoff, but upon moving the physical head, I received the mental suggestion to get up and make this record .

After returning

The clock showed 9:42 p.m. It is interesting to note how the duration of the consecutive projections seemed to have taken longer than they actually did. Perhaps this was due to the intense extraphysical activity during the whole period. I remained lucid from the time I went to bed until now, and the act of awakening was virtually dispensed with.

Observations

By far, the most difficult and impressive part of projection is the moment of lucid takeoff from the waking state. There is no animic or psychic phenomenon that provides a greater impact. It is the one event able to provoke modification of scientific, moral and religious points of view, and has deep, far reaching effects on anyone's knowledge, opinions, education, customs and beliefs. Upon experiencing the lucid takeoff from the soma, generations of teachings are humbled, centuries of civilization are reduced to dust in the mind of the projector, and mountains of prejudice lose their meaning. Through personal experimentation, one dismisses all tiresome arguments. The result is peaceful certainty.

The experience of finding oneself projected with strength and confidence free from the restrictions of the soma, in the same places where we shower, eat, sleep and otherwise live while in the soma is indescribable. It is an invaluable experience, no matter how many times it occurs, and constitutes an important preview of the unavoidable transition of biological death – the final projection. With this preparation, the ghosts and nightmares of the extraphysical dimension vanish forever.

---

33. THE DONORS OF LIFE

Prior to projection

Wednesday, October 17, 1979. Second sleep at 9:02 p.m. Temperature: 77° F. Humidity: 65%. I laid down on the left side.

Extraphysical period

I was fully lucid, following behind three extraphysical females as they entered an enormous extraphysical institution in a monumental building with thick, closed doors. It was dark there. This institution is located somewhere in the crustal dimension, close to human areas, and perhaps above the troposphere.

The ambiance gradually improved as we went down various deserted halls, opening, passing through and closing three doors in succession as we went. All this occurred while in near darkness, immersed in absolute silence.

The third area we reached had a much friendlier feeling, being filled with a tranquilizing light. An impressive spectacle began just after the group entered. In the immense room, resembling an impeccably clean nursery with a high ceiling and white beds, dozens of "women" began to sing an adorable chant of happiness that began with a vibrant refrain:

"Sister souls! Here we are! The donors of life!"

The marvelous, collective *song-prayer*, a mental dialogue of pure emotions, was sung by the extraphysical females of indescribable beauty. Their image comprised a picture difficult to describe. They were dressed in white, the majority of them simply sitting on the beds in the environment, that was criss-crossed with multicolored images.

Energy surged out from the eyes, thoraxes and hands of the singers. These surges of energy became more intense moment by moment, were synchronized to the rhythm of the chant, creating an awesome scenery of multifaceted reflections. Finally, an abundance of sapphire rays poured out in all directions. I almost began singing the enchanting melody that instilled an indescribable sense of well-being and euphoria in all present, the extent of which perhaps only these females could appreciate.

These non-human voices expressed the most elevated feelings. The energies were irresistible. I felt like becoming a child once again and allowing myself to be overtaken by the refrain of the lullaby. It seemed like spring within the walls of the extraphysical construction, where the illumination gradually increased, as the voices became louder. For the first time, I contemplated a crowd of beautiful "women," I had never seen before – true translucent Madonnas and angelic beings – without the slightest thought of sex. Questions arose within me.

"Who was who in this assembly? Which were extraphysical consciousnesses and which ones were projected? Were some of them pregnant?"

The rain of luminous effects did not allow me to perceive the difference. An explanation was transmitted to me. The extraphysical consciousnesses on the beds were preparing for their own rebirth and would eventually become mothers. The anthem of praise to motherhood was being sung by all, including many projected women who would receive others as their children in intraphysical life. There were only female extraphysical consciousnesses participating in the grand chorus, in a celebration of the mothers that would receive the daughters, and who would themselves become heroines of motherhood in the near future. This organization works to renew the more somber areas of the undeveloped extraphysical dimensions, while simultaneously preparing for upcoming intraphysical lives.

I was sincerely surprised to find myself in this extraphysical work group composed of and directed by several profoundly feminine extraphysical "women." They were deeply involved with the sentiments of motherhood, in an institution specializing in the matter. The elevated nature of the ambiance transformed the extraphysical nursery into a sanctuary divided only by the bluish flames. The chant that was being repeated would have brought tears of joy to even the most insensitive individual. My emotional state did not allow me to recall and faithfully report the indescribable lyrics and melody, the eagerness of the feminine chorus, the energetic waves produced by the subtle bodies, the sonorous tenderness spread by the voices and the changes of the colors in the prodigious rain of lights that rained down from above.

It was an unimaginable siren's chant that was being sung. It was impossible for me to hold back the tears of joy brought on by the sweetness of the voices which soon provoked the admonitory discomfort of the call to return to the physical base.

Finding myself in a state of exaltation that was nearly impossible to tolerate, I was not able to recall all the details of the extraphysical events. It was a shame, because I have always wanted to know in which conditions the pregnant-projector carries, along with her, that consciousness who is a candidate for intraphysical life.

After returning

The psychosoma entered the soma from the side in an imposed return. As I awoke, the eyes wet with tears, I could still hear the chant echoing in the twilight of the bedroom. The clock showed 9:57 p.m.

Observations

Just like the emotionalism I experienced in the above projection, one can experience small, harmless extraphysical shocks that can provoke an emotional reaction in the beginning projector. Some examples are: passing the extraphysical hand through a physical object, passing through walls or humans, observing one's own inanimate soma up close, seeing one's psychosoma reflected in a mirror, quick takeoffs from the soma, hearing the intracranial sounds related to a sudden return to the soma, meticulous examination of the silver cord, expansion of consciousness and the visual perceptions, seeing oneself projected in a partially formed psychosoma, sensing the exact moment of the loss of respiration, free flight, extraphysical euphoria, encountering a deceased friend or relative, suffering an attack from a psychotic post-mortem, experiencing transcended time-space continuum with super lucidity, and others. The level of the above extraphysical events is always determined by the quality of the projective experiments.

When I insist that the projector avoid emotionalism and mysticism while executing projective tasks, I am not recommending that he or she turn into a cold, insensitive individual without emotions, feelings, or affection. I am, personally, quite disarmed by the sweetness of the mature consciousness, the simple jest of a child, the sight of a beautiful landscape, the contemplation of a work of art, or a passage in a musical play. The truth, however, is that, in the extraphysical dimension, an emotional state of mind has always proven counterproductive to extraphysical observation.

34. INFLUENCE OF A PERSON

Prior to projection

Saturday, October 20, 1979. New moon at 11:24 p.m. Second sleep at 10:05 p.m. I laid on the stomach and the left side of the face. Temperature: 75° F. Humidity: 66%.

Extraphysical period

I began to awaken during an upwards takeoff through the back, while I was trying to adjust the position of the soma. I returned to the soma and then instantly took off again.

I immediately noticed a male extraphysical consciousness. He was no one that I knew. He appeared to be about 50 years old, with light brown skin. He was short, quite lethargic and seemed to be trying to settle down inside my apartment to go to sleep. Young Arthur had been disturbed by his presence and had called his mother repeatedly since he had gone to bed at 7:00 p.m.

As I came face to face with the "man," still not fully lucid myself, I got the impression that he was a harmless extraphysical consciousness with no specific intentions. I saw several people through the window, at a distance, in the living room of an apartment on a high floor of a nearby building, sitting happily at their table, as if they were having dinner. Astonished by the change in the perspective, the clearness of the features of the neighbors' faces left me certain that I was projected. I suddenly became more lucid.

Soon after approaching the sleepy consciousness, I noticed that he was actually an intraphysical consciousness. I tried to wake him up with these thoughts:

" Hey, my friend, we are in a projection! Wake-up! Go home!"

He had a well composed human form. He was dressed in pants and a sports shirt and continued to exhibit a vague, distracted look, not seeming to understand anything. One can see that even the extraphysical somnambulant can mentally create his own clothing so as to not be projected in the nude. My only recourse was to take him outside with me in an attempt to awaken him. Firmly using all my mental force, but treating him like a novice to extraphysical reality, I took him, saying:

" Look how I fly like Superman!"

My flight with my projected cargo was short, difficult and brief. We flew out of the window and returned immediately.

I went out of the apartment again, this time alone, to see what would happen. As I left easily this time, several extraphysical consciousnesses who knew me emerged from various places. The projected "man" watched my flights and finally disappeared next to the closed window of the living room, while he contemplated the locale in a disoriented fashion. High up from where I flew, I was certain that he had left, and I relaxed.

A lucid, but transfigured and pitiful looking, extraphysical consciousnesses approached me to make an extraphysical attack. I lew away with that consciousness adhered to my psychosoma, gliding over the N. S. da Paz Square, until we reached the driveway of a residential garden at the border of Rodrigo de Freitas Lagoon. There, I left it with another extraphysical consciousness that had appeared next to a green wall. I made no comment. I did not see the sleepy projected consciousness who must have come from one of the apartment buildings in the neighborhood, where his soma doubtless remained sleeping.

I sensed the intangible presence of the helpers, particularly at the point when my extraphysical vision improved, as well as at the door of the lagoon-side residence. I quickly returned to the soma.

After returning

I examined the clock. It was 10:16 p.m. As usual, I had almost completely lost sense of time during the projection. I consulted my wife who confirmed that the projection had lasted 5 minutes. She was able to calculate the projection's duration as she had gone to see our son Arthur in the next room right after talking to me. I was able to recall the projection in its entirety as I awoke.

Observations

Once again, having to deal with consciousnesses that disturb the extraphysical ambiance had helped my projective capacity. These cases act as a kind of catalyst, stimulating one's extraphysical perceptions. The helpers know what they are doing when they let the projector solve certain problems in the projection by himself. These lessons serve to stimulate initiative and nimbleness in the tasks performed while outside the soma.

The act of looking at the event in the distance served to increase my lucidity in the extraphysical dimension. In my projections as a youth, I had failed to observe that heightened visual capacity stimulates the further awakening of the projected consciousness. This represents a recent realization and is a result of a set of projections in series.

What attracted the unidentified projected intraphysical consciousness to the apartment? We can see from the night's occurrences that one can be projected in the condition of a somnambulant or zombie, acting as a crash-projector. In this state, like that of the daydream experienced in the waking state, one becomes profoundly self-absorbed, to the point of not realizing what is happening in one's immediate surroundings.

To what degree does the tendency of being a crash-projector predispose one to behave in the same way even after discarding the soma upon biological death? The projector never gets lost, always eventually returning to the soma through the action of the silver cord. He also always awakens when he or she wishes.

There are psychological and physical characteristics that contribute towards the profile of the ideal projector: iron-clad will; interest in new things; curiosity; lack of religious, scientific and social conditioning; a rational and non-mystical temperament; patient non-conformism; calmness when relating to others; a good memory; studiousness; humanist interests; demanding of him or herself; dynamic but self-controlled; introspective with mental discipline; physical self-control; capable of advanced relaxation.

The finishing touches on the ideal projector are: a singular sexual partner; use of a single bed for projective experiments; always lies down in the dorsal position on a springless bed; performance of projective experiments between midnight and 4 o'clock in the morning (in the second half of the night's sleep); low cardiac frequency; not worried about the next day's issues. I have tried to include at least some of these characteristics, or "tools of the trade," in my personal makeup – a task which has not been easy.

35. MENTAL AUTOMATISM

Prior to projection

Thursday, October 25, 1979. Third sleep, in the dorsal position at 12:34 a.m. I went to sleep alone with the bedroom door shut, after switching off the air conditioner. A little while earlier, I had left my wife, who was laying down in our son's bedroom. He had come down with an ear infection, for which he had received some medication. Temperature: ·77°F. Humidity: 60%. Fair weather.

Extraphysical period

I awoke, little by little, in the bedroom and found myself, still half asleep, heading towards the bedroom of my ailing son. He was my target person. It is common for the projector, once outside of the soma, to head straight for the place where his or her concerns are focused, in an automatic continuation of the actions performed before going to sleep.

Upon reaching my son's bedroom, it occurred to me that my wife should go with the child into the apartment's living room as it is larger and would be more comfortable for the sick little one.

I attempted to communicate my thought to the two of them. In a few minutes, I was in the living room when my wife walked in carrying the child and set him down on one of the couches.

I witnessed their presence in the living room for a few moments, and then went back to the bedroom.

Upon returning to bed, the psychosoma did not immediately re-enter the soma. The psychosoma remained lying on top of the soma, as if it were resting in a peaceful sleep at a height above the soma of about 24", like a captive, stationary balloon attached to the soma.

I did not notice any extraphysical consciousnesses in the apartment during this projection.

For a few moments, I experienced a more-or-less coherent mixture of illusion and reality. I eventually slid into the soma and woke up.

After returning

The soma remained in the same dorsal position in which it had fallen asleep. I gradually recalled having seen my wife and son go into the living room. I got out of bed in order to find out what had actually happened with a great sense of curiosity.

Everything was confirmed. My wife was in the living room with the child who was now lying on one of the couches, crying. Upon asking her, she informed me that she had gone to the living room with the little one 20 minutes before. The clock now showed 1:02 a.m. Elisabeth also told me that it had been Arthur's idea to move to the living room. For the first time in that apartment, both spent the better part of the night in the living room.

Observations

As usual, the projection allowed experimental confirmation of events experienced first-hand while projected in the psychosoma. It is interesting to note that my concern regarding my son's physical condition had caused many actions performed while in the extraphysical dimension to appear to occur in "slow motion." I had also displayed attitudes and mannerisms foreign to my temperament.

Profound lessons can be learned from the above facts. Earthly concerns prevent the achievement of full extraphysical lucidity, due to undisciplined thinking habits. I had already made this observation some time ago during other projections. A fixed dominant concern had kept other extraphysical facts from being registered in my memory.

The dorsal position favors the occurrence of sleep outside of the body. The psychosoma separates from the soma and floats above it in a parallel position. Extraphysical sleep works in conjunction with the projector's technical development, allowing him greater mobility within the reduced parameter of the silver cord's strong attraction.

The little one, who was not quite 5 years old at the time, was able to receive my telepathic suggestion to move to the other room. Up to the physical age of 7, we demonstrate a greater psychic sensitivity to the extraphysical dimension.

If I was able to induce a response to the telepathic suggestion sent to my son while in an out-of-body state, others can do the same. This can also be done with negative intentions. And herein lies the explanation of the cases of morbid intrusion effected against individuals. This unfortunately corroborates the veracity of the negative investment suggestions reported in chapter 26.

Projection is a fact that expands science and religion's scope of influence, enabling those interested in doing so to strike out at the structure of governments. The lucid projection of the consciousness can function as an incredibly powerful resource against which no reasonably effective defense has ever been established. And no one can prevent citizens from sleeping...

The projection of the consciousness outside of the body constitutes an instrument more powerful than the hydrogen bomb. It is fortunate that the cosmoethic and the helpers supervise the projective development of all.

36. A WINGED CARAVAN

Prior to projection

Saturday, October 27, 1979. Temperature: 78°F. Humidity: 69%. I went to bed at 7:22 p.m. I performed energy exercises for about fifteen minutes and then assumed the dorsal position. I then received the telepathic suggestion from a helper to project myself. The strong rhythm of the drums of the samba school in the nearby Morro do Cantagalo noisily penetrated the closed bedroom.

Extraphysical period

I became lucid as soon as the psychosoma took off. I felt it necessary to straighten out the soma. I quickly returned to the soma and opened the legs, placing each one on top of a pillow. Throughout this adjustment the arms did not move and I did not perceive them. It was as if the soma had no arms.

I took off once again, this time with a helper, Tao Mao, who I had known for a long time. It was he who had given me the message prior to the first takeoff. He is an expert on multidimensional activities. He is a supreme mesmerizer with a profound knowledge of psychophysiological issues. He has been my friend since we met through the Casa do Cinza in the city of Uberaba, two decades ago. Tao Mao explained that we would meet up with a multidimensional team that was going to assist persons during a certain human regional celebration.

We flew across a vast distance. The speed of the trip did not allow a detailed observation of the scenes and environments passed.

Soon, we stopped in a rural area in the middle of a field planted with what appeared to be rice. The field was in the foothills of a mountain. It was interesting that the atmosphere appeared to be calm. I concluded that I must be in a distant country, where the seasons and time zone are different from those in Brazil, as night had already fallen over Rio de Janeiro.

I waited with the helper for the arrival of the assistential team. I was instructed to go and pay fraternal respects to the leader of the extraphysical consciousnesses, introducing myself as a member of the projectiology team.

Moments later, I was ecstatic to perceive an approaching cluster of consciousnesses looking like shining low-flying birds coming in the direction of the hill. There is no human event that compares to this indescribably majestic spectacle.

It was impressive to watch them land in an orderly and silent manner, as if it were a procession of pilgrims, all dressed like Lamas or simple monks wearing slightly luminescent hoods. They were magnificent with their radiant psychosomas. As I walked towards them, on Tao Mao's generous urging, a strong consciential force descended from above. We advanced towards each other with open arms, in a fraternal greeting having a wonderful sentiment of peace. We were all under the influence of the incessant torrent of energy which emanated from an indefinable source.

After greeting and embracing the extraphysical consciousnesses at the head of the winged caravan who had now removed their hoods, I could get a close look at their oriental eyes and snow-white hair. They emanated a pale golden glow that shined over the field which was populated with perhaps a hundred of Tao Mao's friends. I felt an extraordinary transfusion of energy coming from the extraphysical consciousnesses. Their penetrating luminous gazes indicated that I should proceed up the hill.

It was possible to fly at high altitudes in this area, but I was only gliding some 26 feet above the ground while climbing the sprawling mountain to a construction similar to a border monument. As I approached, it was possible to see some people gathered around the structure, many wearing wide conical black hats. I noticed illegible inscriptions on the monument and a faint internal illumination when I finally reached it. The location was overflowing with visitors.

I was able to tell that I was in China. Various extraphysical consciousnesses observed the caravan glide up the hill a few yards off the ground. The place appeared quite similar to Hong Kong, where I had visited more than a decade before. The extraphysical consciousnesses attended a few moments of the solemn proceedings that were taking place on the hill. Then they gradually dispersed to perform assistential work that was being organized in small teams. These teams were to work in a studious manner, in the intraphysical dimension. It became clear to me that extraphysical assistance occurs everywhere, and that lucid consciousnesses congregate in the most diverse extraphysical regions in order to work towards furthering evolution.

I left and passed by a house that was close to the other side of the hill. I observed a boy who was playing with an instrument he had in his hand. I passed through the house, saw his mother working in the kitchen and left through a rustic gate that opened to the fenced yard. I went down a path that passed through several trees and, now in full flight, willed myself to glide at a higher level. It was now time to return from the projection, and I soon arrived alone at the physical base.

After returning

Upon awakening, the soma, which was in the dorsal position with its spread legs on top of pillows, felt like it was made of steel.

As I moved the arms of the soma, I heard the apparently dehydrated fingers make cracking noises. While the entire soma was stiff, it was immersed in a pleasant shower of powerful vibrations.

As I awoke, I recalled the extraphysical events in their entirety, and realized the need to record the events. The clock showed 8:57 p.m.

37. THE RESOUNDING VOICE

Prior to projection

Thursday, November 1, 1979. Temperature: 75°F when the local air conditioner was switched off. Humidity: 60%. Fair weather. I went to bed at 7:30 p.m. and laid in the dorsal position, physically relaxed. I immediately began energy emission exercises.

Extraphysical period

I became aware that I was projected as I left the apartment with the target idea of finding a place with switches in order to try turning lights on and off.

As soon as I had the idea, a resounding clarification echoed close by, as if it were inside my head. It addressed the fact that when we think, we create. I heard:

"There is a difference between physical objects and the creations of your mind. This bag of toys, for example, is a mental creation."

Close to my hand, a bag appeared. It seeming to be full of toys, like the bags used by Santa Clauses at Christmas parties.

"You can pick it up and throw it. If you so desire, the noise of the bag hitting the floor can also be created, but it all represents a creation of the mind."

As I picked up the bag, I thought it would make a noise. As it hit the cement floor, it made a "tap" sound. The voice continued:

"The physical objects you see are real and are outside of your soma. Let's see if you can sharpen your extraphysical vision."

At that moment, it seemed that everything instantly obeyed the thought. My extraphysical vision became quite amplified and I had the desire to move further away. It is necessary to be aware and gradually create extraphysical reflexes, in order to better control the psychosoma while outside of the body.

I could see a wide door in an apparently deserted dimly lit street. I wanted to go through the door and immediately found myself doing so. I was now on another street, next to a large warehouse similar to those in the dock area of Rio de Janeiro's seaport. Now gliding and totally lucid, I discovered a few light switches in the dark warehouse. As I neared them, I again heard the explanation:

"You think that you switched the light on. It seems to you as though you have, but you really haven't. Try to observe: what you think of happens, because the will desires it to be so. But the will is only able to affect the extraphysical dimension that you are in right now and not the intraphysical dimension that you are seeing and are appearing to touch, but are really not affecting."

Upon sharpening my extraphysical attention so as not to compromise my perceptions, everything happened as predicted when I attempted to move the switches. I firmly felt the movement of the switches on the wall. It seemed that I had touched and switched them all into the "on" position; however, the lights did not turn on. The action had merely been simulated. The resounding voice said:

"Do not concern yourself with moving physical objects. In order to do that, you would need to expend a lot more of your energies, while your extraphysical body is in a much denser state."

I was not able to see or thank the owner of this resounding voice at any time during the projection. Only with greater experience is the projector able to discern when he or she is in fact seeing physical objects with clarity and when he or she is adding his own morphothosenes based on his perception. Thought is an extraordinarily forceful creative resource. If the projected mind thinks that a detail is missing in an object, it can immediately add it, including it in its perceptions.

Gliding down the street, I reached its end and saw several people walking on the sidewalk in the distance. As I glided on, invisible to the pedestrians, I received a suggestion to return to the soma. I awakened immediately upon returning.

After returning

The soma was still in the dorsal position. The clock showed 8:27 p.m. I got out of bed to write down my clear recollection of the profound comments made by the resounding voice.

Observations

We can see that conscious projection infinitely expands the boundaries of reality. A whole new world, larger than the physical one, has been discovered and awaits exploration.

Simulation of action, as illustrated above, frequently occurs when one is dreaming while projected in the psychosoma or, in other words, when in the transitional phase between a common dream and a conscious projection.

38. INSPIRATIONAL ASSISTANCE

Prior to projection

Friday, November 2, 1979. All Souls Day. Third sleep at 11:17 p.m. Temperature: 73°F. Indirect air conditioning. I laid on the left side.

Upon going to bed for the first sleep of the night, at 7:11 p.m., extensive energy emission exercises were performed, including a lucid takeoff of the psychosoma, that remained in the close proximity of the soma for quite some time before returning. It seemed that a more extensive preparation was needed for upcoming projections.

Extraphysical period

I became lucid beside a helper who explained the night's tasks. This time we were going to experience an extended excursion to various distant places, taking into account the schedules of human activities. The helper did not geographically identify the places where we would be going.

It would be important to maintain an alert mind and good powers of observation in order to be able to later make note of the extraphysical events. Priority was to be given to the registration of more important events. Excessive attention to detail has a negative effect on the accuracy of the recollections.

It was in fact a long voyage, similar to a few that I had experienced before. I have summarized the principle events experienced given the natural limitations that affect the process.

At the entrance of a building in its final stages of construction, the extraphysical consciousness who was leading the way explained that a vocational school that would accept hundreds of students was being installed.

The building appeared to have four floors. The top one was a vast recreation area with ramps and a gymnasium, all protected by high walls. The lower floors were equipped with areas for technical work and looked like machine shops. The essential attribute of the school appeared to be the extraphysical preparation of the environment, taking into account the future human workers.

The helper introduced me to the assistential team that would be responsible for the extraphysical monitoring to be performed once the school was fully operative. The extraphysical consciousness who had inspired the undertaking of and had lent his name to the project worked alongside the others. They were preparing the environment with the dedication of church caretakers, cleansing the extraphysical environment, provoking intuitive inspiration in the human workers, and setting up local lines of defense, among other things. They were establishing an invisible foundation that appeared to be more detailed than the floor plans drawn up for the physical institution.

After visiting the school construction, we went on to look at various types of factories in several distant locations. One factory in particular stood out as it had placed an emphasis on the minute details of the multidimensional services that were being implemented in the organization. I somehow felt that it was very distant from Brazil.

I was astounded to see the degree of intraphysical and extraphysical monitoring going on in the different work areas, some of them active at that time. I could see that the surveillance and security systems were networked throughout the various key areas, all of which were being continuously monitored by the omnipresent gaze of closed-circuit cameras connected to a central room equipped with ample viewing screens and around-the-clock vigilance. Panels of monitors showing images of all work stations were mounted on the walls.

The extraphysical consciousness explained that the zealously prepared physical precautions reflected only a small fraction of the enthusiasm of the extraphysical councilors who were in charge of preventing physical accidents as well as external interference by "shadowy" consciousnesses upon the unwary workers. In this way, they would prevent disasters that could bring unpredictable consequences.

Our exploration continued. From the community power plant to the huge food processing plant supplying a massive population. From an apparently insignificant school still under construction to university laboratories. From a backyard factory to an industrial park. It all demanded the silent dedication, the tireless, steadfast protection, and the tenderness and inspiration of evolved extraphysical consciousnesses.

Leaders of large physical establishments can be absolutely sure that they never work alone, even though their board rooms may appear deserted. Extraphysical consciousnesses are everywhere minimizing problems, smoothing out rough edges, inspiring workers and moving things in a fraternal direction.

There is an extraphysical personnel department in every large establishment on the planet. If this were not the case, the number of problems and accidents in business establishments would increase geometrically to terrifying proportions. There are tasks everywhere for the extraphysical consciousness that works on the planetary crust.

The assistance provided by evolved extraphysical consciousnesses can be felt from the noblest programs down to the most humble and apparently uncivilized human activities. Well intentioned human collaborators arduously work in all conceivable areas, and deserve assistance in order to minimize any setbacks they may suffer.

It was impossible for me to hide the thoughts that came to mind of, among other things, the huge slaughter houses that sacrifice animals for human consumption; the powerful armament and munitions factories dedicated to the production of police resources and the sustaining of wars, which have spread throughout the planet like never before in human history; and controversial nuclear power plants which, in spite of allegedly existing for the safety and comfort of the population, have caused long-time dissatisfaction and discomfort to persons throughout the world. This illustrates the current evolutionary level of human population.

Everything is under the control of the basic directives of constantly wakeful multidimensional work forces. Workers should always trust in the presence of inspirational extraphysical assistants. To be a part of a community service team is also to evolve. Through this participation, we acquire talents and perseverance through our efforts, resulting in lasting accomplishments.

All great personalities at the forefront of human thought, have punched many time cards during several of their previous lives. The well established 20-year-old factory did not appear overnight; nor was it created without inspiration from the higher spheres. In the roots of every great tree of human progress, runs the sap of the silent, anonymous abnegation of extraphysical teams. To reflect upon and understand humans with their contradictions, paradoxes, crises, struggles and sacrifices made on the path of inner growth, seems always to be one of the more difficult consciential accomplishments. Everyone who is reborn participates in human life compulsorily. All who participate are inevitably burdened by human needs, many of which appear to be diametrically opposed to each other. The responsibilities and the challenge of living righteously while inside a vehicle of flesh and bones among other humans is ever increasing.

As we left the last organization, where workers were in full activity, a psychotic post-mortem approached the helper and could not be ignored due to its demeanor. The psychosoma of the extraphysical consciousness had large, bright red marks throughout. Its hair appeared to have been combed for the occasion. The forehead, face, arms, hands and legs had large blood-colored blemishes on them. Judging from the tenderness with which it was attended, I could tell that it had worked in the establishment some time ago. Its condition was symptomatic of a pathology of the mentalsoma. A subtle intuition informed me that its condition was a consequence of exposure to atomic radiation while in the physical body – a condition that had continued beyond biological death. After observing the ailing extraphysical consciousness, I began the lengthy return to the physical base.

After returning

As I opened the eyes, while under a thin bedspread, the soma lying on the left side seemed frozen with the peaceful rigidity of a cadaver. Fragments of the extraphysical events came to me, maintaining the consistency of various thoughts, judgments and sensations, as though I had just finished watching a long movie. It is very difficult to have total recall of the multifaceted events experienced in projections of long duration at long distances. The sharpness of the images of scenes and personalities encountered while projected is always very impressive. I will never forget the faces of certain workers who were interviewed that night.

The clock showed 2:27 a.m. The projection had lasted more than three hours, without any sensation of time having been compressed. A light rain continued to fall over Ipanema. After calmly recording the events witnessed, it was 4:31 a.m. I was not able to go back to sleep again.

39. *INSTRUCTIVE JOURNEY*

Prior to projection

Friday, November 9, 1979. An atypical day. Temperature in the bedroom: 75°F. Relative humidity: 55%. Second sleep at 2:04 a.m., lying on the right side. It had rained that evening. Intraphysical state: final stages of convalescence from colitis; still under medication; no fever.

I had performed brief energy exercises with the soma earlier in the dorsal position, while still in the waking state, after doing some work in the living room. These included self-energization while coupled with an extraphysical consciousness. It was now just after midnight on Thursday.

Extraphysical period

After some forty minutes of concentration, a rapid projection occurred. I emerged with the psychosoma in the horizontal position, floating above the soma and oscillating slightly as if it were a feather or a soap bubble in mid air. After a few brief moments, as I tried to stand up, the soma called me with an energetic tug of the silver cord. Once more, I heard the unique intracranial sounds, that seemed like a short "creak" made by a cabinet door closing with difficulty. As I had always observed, the extraphysical sensations were very sharp and vivid, although much more delicate than their intraphysical counterparts. The speed of the violent re-entry broke the projective trance quite abruptly.

I then awoke outside the soma between two young-looking extraphysical friends in the multidimensional team. Moments into our instructive journey, we were entering an area surrounding a large city that was clearly not Rio de Janeiro. The higher ranking extraphysical consciousness made reference to the difficulty of flying over certain urban areas that appear to possess geomagnetic currents that make the process of flight extremely difficult. This may have been due to an increase in the weight of the psychosoma – particularly in the case of a projector.

I recalled that the psychosoma, even though it is "more subtle" and does not breathe air, is still slightly material or physical in nature. It has been stated that it should weigh about one thousandth of the weight of the soma. So, a person weighing 154 pounds would have a psychosoma weighing approximately 2.5 ounces.

The soma is referred to as the "human body," as it is denser. But it is still a vehicle of manifestation of the consciousness, as it presents the silver cord even when inanimate, during a projection, as well as presenting the aura and psychosoma when the bodies are in alignment. Also, when one discards the soma while passing through the first death, the holo-chakra or energetic body is not yet completely discarded. In this state, the psychosoma remains fairly dense, retaining a varying, minimal percentage of energy. Words do not always faithfully represent the reality of a situation.

The helper, wanting to illustrate the difficulty of flying while in this condition, indicated that I should climb up a tree-covered hill on which I saw a few castor oil and other plants. I climbed the hill with great difficulty. The psychosoma felt very heavy. It was as if it were filled with rocks. What is the influence of gravity in this case?

As I reached the top, the extraphysical consciousness commented mentally in good humor:

"And now, would you like to descend flying?"

Neither my companion nor myself wished to take the risk, so we went down in a low-level glide. What would be the consequences of a flying descent for the psychosoma?

As I left the base of the hill, I observed various canals dividing the streets and surrounding area. Some of them had lighted streetlights on their banks that reflected off the surface of the water.

Upon passing in front of a residential area, I saw water gushing out at several spots in the middle of the asphalt, suggesting the existence of broken water pipes. The leading extraphysical consciousness decided to wait for the repair crew in order to avoid a greater calamity in the locale, because the principal junction in the network feeding the whole area was located not far from there.

Moments later, repair crews arrived and went straight to work. Two extraphysical consciousnesses instantly established a kind of energetic defense encircling them. They went as far as inspiring one of the workers, perhaps the foreman, by placing one hand on top of the head and the other before the frontal-chakra, transmitting ideas to him. Minutes later, the water stopped gushing out. A small number of extraphysical spectators followed the repair process as it unfolded. The asphalt was not going to be immediately repaired, but the critical danger had been contained.

The same two extraphysical consciousnesses called me to leave. As we glided away from the area, various other extraphysical consciousnesses commented on our exit. The lead extraphysical consciousness requested that we not engage in mental dialogue.

A little later, we entered a colonial style house where a respectable looking gentleman of about 55 years of age was totally absorbed in the massive volume he was reading. The leader of our group chased two psychotic post-mortems away, who had been beside him. Upon approaching the gentleman, the extraphysical consciousness endeavored to impart some constructive suggestions to him regarding the topic that he was studying.

I observed that the man was mentally immersed in a volume of criminal law. The case he was studying concerned a victim with a knife wound in his back. In the gentleman's thoughts I saw images alluding to perceived death, premature burial, similar precedent cases, a theatrical play, and difficulties in the trial. Several volumes lay on top of the lawyer's desk. It was late at night and I noticed that the room had a pleasant ambient temperature.

Eventually the man got up, apparently with the intention of taking a drink of some beverage in the back of the residence. There was a car in the garage and a guard dog sleeping in the inner patio.

At this point, the helpers thought it best that I return to the physical base. The legal case was not discussed between us, and I did not ask about it, maintaining my usual discretion. One can see from this night's events that the tasks undertaken by extraphysical consciousnesses are infinitely diverse.

After returning

Upon waking up in the soma which was lying on the right side, I recalled the extraphysical events in a fragmentary but consistent and connected fashion. The clock showed 3:27 a.m. Heavy rain drops drummed on the cover of the air conditioner. I could occasionally hear the echo of cars passing over thick metal plates on some nearby street under construction.

40.   EVOLUTION IN GROUP

Prior to projection

Wednesday, November 14, 1979. Second sleep at 9:08 p.m., lying on the right side. Ambient temperature, 77° F. Indirect air conditioning coming from the study. Humidity: 65%. Fair weather.

Extraphysical period

I was perfectly aware of being projected, when I tranquilly appeared among several extraphysical friends of mine. They had all been spiritists in intraphysical life and were amiably exchanging ideas over tasks on earth.

Some of the more relaxed ones were playing while others were telling "intermissive jokes" or jokes about the intermissive period (extraphysical intermission between intraphysical lives). One of the stories related telepathically by an extraphysical consciousness having a full head of gray hair, referred to the "extraphysical beauty parlor." Most consciousnesses go through this beauty parlor when they return to the extraphysical dimension.

"There are true 'mummies' automatically resuscitated into young bucks in the 'rejuvenation parlor'."

A more experienced extraphysical consciousness mentally told me seriously:

"You can be sure that projection is a capacity inherent in everyone. It is a reality accessible to anyone with some degree of discipline. The ability to control the projection of the consciousness depends on one's ability to control their own thoughts, judgments, wishes, emotions, motivations and affinities."

Someone made a comment about the "intraphysical team" that was preparing to meet with an extraphysical team that would accompany persons to a debate beginning the following day in Rio de Janeiro. The debate would bring journalists and spiritist authors together from all over Brazil, under the auspices of the Brazilian Spiritist Federation.

Extraphysical consciousnesses began arriving either before or along with the humans that would speak at the debate. The fraternal gathering had a cordial extraphysical atmosphere.

I was requested to visit a dear friend. I left the gathering with three other companions.

Our arrival at this other area, also in the intraphysical dimension, was met with a great deal of fraternal celebration. One extraphysical consciousness who was already there when we arrived, referred to the various types of existential programs that were assigned to individuals during their series of intraphysical lives.

There are groups that "fly like an eagle." Others "go by the book." Still others live to "punch time clocks," and so on. At that point, the extraphysical consciousness W. got together with C., B., E., M., and others, some of which were related due to their existential tasks (tasks in physical life), having been involved in the same mission during physical life. First initials were used here at the recommendation of the helpers.

In this unrepressed atmosphere, devoid of mysticism or backwardness, I requested "something" that I might be able to take with me upon my return to the soma. They all implied that Eurípedes Barsanulfo, my great benefactor since childhood, was present in order to transmit some ideas to me.

Concentrating while shoulder to shoulder with me, he expressed his thoughts on *evolution in group* in more or less the following terms:

"The withholding of ideas should be observed and considered in our relationships with others.

We have all been in and will all return to the intraphysical condition. When we appear in a human family as a father, mother, brother, or sister, we need to fraternally accept to live in this family together with: the balanced as well as the unbalanced consciousnesses; the calm as well as agitated individuals; the studious and also the negligent ones; the intellectuals and those less brilliant; the easygoing fellows and those who are more difficult to get along with.

We are encouraged neither by life nor by nature to shut out those individuals needing the most extraphysical assistance, even though they may not meet our standards. On the contrary, these companions are almost always the reason why we are called upon to be reborn into specific conditions.

The natural order of life dictates that we must not exclude these individuals, but rather, go forth together with them.

Similarly, we find others with whom we have been specifically petitioned to exercise true fraternity and cooperation.

This necessitates that we not cast them out, but instead, work to motivate them and foster their greater understanding.

For the sake of spiritual truth and fraternal love, it is imperative to join, and not divide.

No one is reborn to evolve with someone 'by chance.'

The pathological thosenes of our comrades can reflect upon us. No advances in the climb to the top can ever be achieved by taking shortcuts. Evolution, whether we like it or not, as well as being an individual process, is also inevitably a group process.

Sometimes it is difficult to understand the mechanics of destiny, but it arises, aiming for the improvement of the consciousnesses in group.

The process of self-evolution does not allow us to forget those individuals who have been left behind.

No one is allowed to ascend to the more advanced dimensions carrying memory lapses in the depths of the consciousness.

We evolve together, rising up hand in hand, and fly into infinity in flocks."

I attentively tried to record the message. I was soon told to return to the physical, which I did. I awoke immediately, recalling the message mentally transmitted by Eurípedes, who I thanked profusely.

After returning

I awoke and consulted the clock. It was 10:04 p.m. My wife soon opened the bedroom door and prepared herself for sleep.

Observations

One can never be sure what will happen in a projection. Nevertheless, there is always a strong correlation between the profile of one's intraphysical life and the events encountered while outside the soma.

41. GUIDED PROJECTIONS

Prior to projection

Friday, November 16, 1979. The thermometer in the bedroom wall indicated 77°F. Air Humidity 61%. Fair weather. I was downtown in the afternoon and intended to stay there until the evening when a helper advised me to go home on account of projective work that was needed. The exercises began at 7:49 p.m. while sitting in bed. I felt the presence of Tao Mao taking total control of my soma while performing energy transmissions from a distance.

For about 20 minutes, during the period of human anguish (6:00-10:00 p.m.), energy work was performed up until the time that the extraphysical consciousness had me lay my soma down in the "dorsal position," and put a fluffy pillow under the head and two others under the knees. The hands were placed on the legs close to the groin. It was as if he was teaching me the ideal physical position for the takeoff of the psychosoma. I returned to the waking state as soon as Tao Mao relinquished the direct control of my dense body. The body began to feel numb, beginning with the hands, arms, feet, legs, and trunk. The numbness finally reached the neck and facial muscles.

An invisible right hand landed on my forehead without affecting my lucidity. I realized it was possible to move the extraphysical arms above the abdomen in a partial separation. I remained lucid for many minutes, as I tried to select a personal system of stronger vibrations more conducive to takeoff. I identified the presence of two friendly extraphysical consciousnesses beside me.

I felt that I was going to have a projection with continuous lucidity with the assistance of the extraphysical consciousness Tao Mao.

Extraphysical period

I had approximately 100% lucidity upon first leaving the body. The psychosoma bobbed slightly until it became stabilized a few inches above the soma. The silver cord then immediately pulled it back. Tao Mao began to work with energy throughout the soma. After a few more minutes he advised me, "Roll to your right."

Obeying, I rolled the psychosoma to the right and made a perfect exit. Remaining close by, I felt the intense force of the energetic cord, as if I were testing it. This connection between the bodies has amazing vigor and power. Conscious takeoff triggers the energetic release of a fabulous power plant within ourselves. Rolling the psychosoma appears to be child's play, but is extremely effective.

Returning to the body, I again received the suggestion to roll to the right. This time the psychosoma rolled to the right three times by itself, with surprising speed and momentum. It is interesting to note that the psychosoma spins freely and does not become tangled with the silver cord. I had previously experienced this unique property of the silver cord during a spiral takeoff.

The environment was brightly illuminated. I flew away profoundly happy. I began to feel a tranquil inner power and an indescribable sensation of non-physicality and lightness. I again experienced the euphoria of extraphysical life, which is incontestably superior to intraphysical existence. This experience leaves one with a feeling of being absolutely at peace with humanity and the entire universe. All of life's setbacks, pain, labors, emotions, aspirations, and efforts all but disappear in light of the multidimensional reality experienced while in the extraphysical dimension. Any human attempt to express this experience does not do it justice.

I intentionally swam through the air using the invisible replica of the human body. This time, not being as dense as usual, I went from one place to another above the Atlantic Ocean, until I received the suggestion from Tao Mao to return to the soma.

I re-entered the soma in tenths-of-a-second and remained perfectly lucid, even though I did not awaken. The cataleptic soma gave me the impression of being like a locked box. I knew that I could very easily project myself from this state into space if I wished. In my particular case, I realized that it is much easier to effect successive takeoffs, after the first lucid takeoff in a series of projections on the same day or night – especially if I don't move the soma between projections.

The serene helper informed me that those operating at high cosmoethical levels are able to be productive and useful in many dimensions. They can gradually attain the state of continuous lucidity, moving uninterruptedly back and forth between the intra-physical and extraphysical dimensions. The cosmoethic serves to build an interdimensional bridge that allows recall of events to pass from one dimension to the other virtually without effort. These individuals eventually live life in a state of continuous wakefulness.

I fully accept this as fact. The great luminaries of evolution initiate the interdimensional bridge in the extraphysical period between intraphysical lives. They dispense with "sleep" while in the extraphysical state, leaving the psychosoma at rest and operating exclusively through the mentalsoma.

The consciousness does not need to sleep. The soma and, in some cases, the psychosoma need sleep. Dreaming is the greatest protest of the consciousness against sleep. Lucid projection represents the victory of the consciousness over sleep and dreams.

After returning

I received a suggestion to move the arms and the whole body. When I moved the soma, several joints cracked. I rolled from the dorsal position onto the left side. I wanted to leave the soma again, but Tao Mao suggested I get up and record my impressions in every detail. This was, after all, the reason that the guided projection had occurred.

The clock showed 9:07 p.m. I got up, went to the living room, called my wife, who was sitting close to one of her relatives watching TV, and told her about the projection. I tried to pass on to her some of the intense happiness I was feeling as a result of the series of projections I had had during the night.

Extraphysical period

Confirming my suppositions, I later had another conscious takeoff, achieved when I rolled the psychosoma to the left. This projection lasted on into the night. I performed assistential tasks at great distances with my friend Tao Mao, who I thanked for all his efforts during the night. I did not experience any sensation of pity during the extraphysical events.

Observations

There are dozens of techniques that allow one to project. The projection that is assisted by a helper, who transmits mental orders, is extraordinarily easy and gives one an inexpressible sense of well being. Experience shows that an effortless projection of this nature generally constitutes a preview for the projector of assistential tasks, that may or may not be remembered. Practicing the lucid departure from and return to the soma is very important, because the more one projects, the fewer exercises are required to reproduce the experience.

Experience acquired from numerous short and seemingly unimportant projections, paves the way for more prolonged and important projections which result from a greater understanding of the processes involved and from the necessary discipline of thoughts, emotions and the psychosoma.

I was lucid from the beginning to the end of the projective cycle. There are perfect and imperfect projections and returns to the soma. Their quality depends upon the degree of lucidity of the consciousness at the various stages of the projection. In the projection related above, I rate myself at maintaining 90% to 100% extraphysical lucidity throughout the projection.

I now felt euphoric and was ready to do things. I have noticed over the past few years, that even projections that last a few minutes stimulate the soma and protect one's physical health. Is this a consequence of extraphysical euphoria? Projection is not at all a mysterious process. It is within the reach of anyone, requiring only a certain degree of personal effort. Projection is, for obvious reasons, especially recommended for those who are blind, paraplegic, have a terminal illness, or are incarcerated, allowing one to temporarily escape from physical fatigue, pain, illness and countless other problems. The projector is able to lead a double life, going anywhere he or she pleases in the liberated psychosoma.

Based on this night's events, I concluded that it is not always possible to separate the passive from the active components during the projection of the psychosoma. The segmented projections of the psychosoma constitute the partial non-alignment of the bodies – a phenomenon which frequently occurs before a full projection. The non-alignment of the bodies predisposes the partial returns to the soma that usually happen in tenths of a second. Partial returns, when sudden, cause regional repercussions in the body. These sudden regional repercussions are strongly connected with the chakras or energetic centers.

The repercussion in the abdominal area, where the sex-chakra (root chakra), umbilical-chakra and splenic-chakra are located, either causes shivers to run up and down the spine, or the contraction of the anal sphincter. A repercussion in the thoracic area, where the cardio-chakra is located, causes a compulsive deep sigh, as it effects the lungs and breathing. A repercussion in the neck area, where the laringeal-chakra (throat chakra) lies, stimulates the sudden, unexpected secretion of saliva. The reentry of the extraphysical head or entire psychosoma, directed by the coronal-chakra (crown chakra) at the top of the head, causes a characteristic crackling noise inside the head, which is the classic sound of an abrupt return to the soma. When a total sudden return to the soma is extremely violent, the projector may experience temporary palpitations, as well as intracranial sounds.

The partial return of the arms and legs of the psychosoma produces motor effects, or contractions and muscular spasms. Sometimes the motor effects are restricted to the fingers or a single isolated finger.

When a small non-alignment of the bodies occurs, it is common for the psychosoma to almost entirely exit the soma, all except for the extraphysical head. The rest of the psychosoma, remains inclined, with the feet being furthest from the soma. In this state, called the Trendelenburg position, the projector remains in the waking state. Soon thereafter, the psychosoma leaves the soma, assuming a dorsal position above it. This type of phenomenon is easily verified by those who have had some projections. The Trendelenburg position can occur while one is in the hypnagogic state, being the preliminary stage of sleep where the non-alignment of the bodies first occurs. In other words, these repercussions may happen to unconscious projectors or to anyone, as the sleep state is being entered.

Upward takeoffs in a spiral manner and those effected through quickly rolling the psychosoma to the side, demonstrate that the silver cord can be twisted without suffering any adverse effects. Could it be that this energetic cord is made up of an agglomeration of energy or a quintessential substance?

42. DAYTIME PROJECTION

Prior to projection

Monday, November 19, 1979. After returning from the bathroom, I consulted the clock: 4:51 a.m. Daylight already flooded Ipanema as if it were already summer. The temperature the day before had reached 100.5°F. I laid down on the left side for the last sleep of the night. The air conditioning was running in the study and the bedroom door was open. I was sleepy. Relative humidity was 52%. Temperature : 77°F. Phase of the moon: New moon at 3:04 p.m.

Extraphysical period

I did not experience the takeoff. I suddenly became aware of the presence of two male-looking extraphysical consciousnesses. They wore impeccably white shirts and uniforms, and appeared to be Americans, with closely cropped hair. I somehow knew that they had spoken English while on Earth. After exchanging fraternal greetings, we left together without further delay. Once again, we traveled too fast to be able to make out anything of any significance along the way. Within moments we reached a tropical area where the sun was so bright that it shined and reflected everywhere.

The primitive area where we found ourselves seemed to be a large island or a continental coastline. I saw short, dark, semi-naked natives. They were scattered about amongst numerous grass huts and trellises. I could tell that they were all busy with preparations for a celebration. Would there be a tribal festivity, a wedding or both? I did not know. The helpers left me alone to take in the scenery while they advanced into the camp. I watched in great detail as some natives prepared a huge bull that had been roasted. Some men and women were covering it with small skewers, which gave the impression of fish scales. Containers filled mostly with coconuts and pineapples were being placed next to it.

I saw rustic huts made of tree branches with roofs of twigs and leaves. Their floors were completely covered with leaves, many of them dried, serving as a carpet for the celebrations. There was a section fenced in like an open air corral which also was carpeted with leaves. Small groups of natives were watching the preparations. The majority were taking part in the arrangements.

I closely observed a man (or woman) dressed from head to toe in a garment made of white ornamental fiber balls. This clothing covered the entire body and part of the face. This person was putting the final touches on their ceremonial robe in preparation for the festivities. Others were preparing similar garments.

In certain places, the corral fences were higher and completely separated the workers from the spectators. Many followed the events while perched on primitive wooden structures. Exotic trees that complemented the sun-bathed scenery could be seen everywhere. There were dozens of semi-nude youngsters. A band of twelve-year-olds was playing together, using leaves to slide down a nearby hill. A lady with dark skin and a limp in her left leg, was being helped by several other young women as she minded a pot containing liquids and herbs. Were those condiments?

The sea waves crashed onto the rocks of the nearby beaches where some palm trees grew. I was observing the preparations while the two extraphysical consciousnesses in white uniforms (had they been navy officers?) removed psychotic postmortems from the area. One of the extraphysical consciousnesses approached me and said that extraphysical assistance is performed wherever it is required. The two extraphysical consciousnesses had a great affection for the inhabitants native to the area, because it was there that they had passed through the first death (discarding of the soma) during a war a long time before.

The extraphysical consciousnesses affirmed that no one lives without the constant observation of multidimensional teams. Not only humans, but animals and plants as well. Everything is under an invisible and subtle control which is difficult for the consciousness to understand in detail while it is in the intraphysical state. Human ties, regardless of their physical, familial, sentimental or intellectual nature, are retained even after biological death, creating lasting energetic connections that one can feel in a relationship.

The extraphysical consciousness explained that members of savage tribes, such as the one before us, would sometimes ingest vegetal concoctions and potions that provoked semi-lucid projections of the psychosoma. These projections would take place in the proximity of their soma. Their mystical beliefs, superstitions, taboos, ridiculous fears and their lifestyle, however devoid of sophistication and hypocrisies, would distort their perceptions during these projections. This distortion would be worsened through their emotional reaction to confronting the unknown. Their inability to observe, study, classify, absorb and carefully experiment with collected facts worsens the situation. Their legends, folklore and magic spells are a product of these experiences.

The extraphysical consciousness explained that the euphoria I feel and sometimes have difficulty in containing is not unlike the reactions of these natives. All emotionalism ends up disturbing one's balance, lucidity, and the *modus operandi* of the psychosoma during a projection. With that in mind, I seriously reflected on the need to avoid negative ideas, and thoughts of sorrow, fear, uncertainty, or pain. I also considered the need to understand the importance of discarding conventional social formulas and redirect affinities and tendencies in favor of the basic principles of evolution.

It is imperative to become more rational and free ourselves from instinctive emotional reactions, realizing that even seemingly positive emotions, such as euphoria, can produce negative results.

One of the extraphysical consciousnesses soon invited me to return to the soma. I expressed my gratitude for the extraphysical ride and the teachings, and bid them farewell. Within moments, I arrived in my bedroom thinking about the energetic affinities that had established multi-existential interrelationships between these more advanced extraphysical military consciousnesses and their illiterate, less civilized comrades.

After returning

The extraphysical events came to me in their entirety as I awoke. It appeared that two well defined lapses of lucidity had occurred: a longer one during takeoff and another that had begun during the return to the soma which ended moments before waking up. The clock showed 5:48 p.m.

This had been a typical daytime projection to a remote location. The sunlight had not seemed to affect the psychosoma. Observations show that sunlight appears to exert some influence on the takeoff process and on the inactive soma. However, sunlight does not effect the psychosoma once it transcends the extraphysical sphere of energy.

I have always observed the importance of extraphysical and human celebrations. Other chapters that deal with celebrations are numbers 16, 29, 33, 36.

43. EXTRAPHYSICAL MUSIC

Prior to projection

Saturday, November 29, 1979. I went to bed to perform energy emission exercises at 8:32 p.m., and remained in the dorsal position for a few minutes until my wife entered the room at 9:26 p.m. to go to sleep. The ambient temperature was 77° F. The bedroom was being cooled with indirect air conditioning. Humidity 55%. Being Saturday night, it was quite noisy in Ipanema. It had been extremely hot during the day, the temperature reaching 100°F. It had rained close to nightfall.

As I initiated energy exercises, I once again perceived several physiological occurrences which contributed to energetic detoxification. Most notable are the successive yawns, tearing, running nose and light coughs. It was as though the helper was washing and drying the breathing pathways in preparation for an immediate projection. This shows that breathing has a noticeable influence on the separation of the psychosoma.

Extraphysical period

I awoke as I entered a familiar extraphysical colony where I re-encountered the extraphysical consciousness Carnot, referred to in Chapter 2. Carnot was a friend and permanent resident of this colony.

The area was similar to a resort on Earth, made up of neat houses scattered throughout a forest which is permeated by soft light. The area was divided by inviting trails and clearings richly carpeted with soft grass. Sublime music penetrated the pleasant environment, affecting all the sensibilities. The music was not audible in the physical sense, and its notes involved and invaded the perceptions as one paid attention to it. If one were to allow him or herself to be swayed by the vibrations and impressions produced by the refined harmony, one would end up dancing, singing or exalting oneself, in accordance with the intensity and irresistible rhythm in the moment, through a spontaneous participation in the eternal, enthusiastic and seductive outdoor concert.

Carnot explained that the delicious sound waves that could be felt but not heard, constituted music therapy taken to the extreme. It is capable of restoring the memory, the imagination and the judgment of extraphysical consciousnesses still traumatized by human experiences. It dissolves conflicts, apprehensions, doubts, regrets, fixed ideas and opinions.

He informed me that there was an extensive number of inhabitants in the colony and that the majority were "convalescing from their biological condition at the time of death," as they had arrived at the extraphysical dimension at an advanced earth age, suffering from senility.

I noticed that Carnot was more intellectually confident. This was the first time I had seen him at this extraphysical colony where he lived and worked, serving the elderly that had recently arrived from the intraphysical dimension. We communicated through thought transmissions without articulating any words. The consciousness, in this case, sends and receives complete ideas.

The good Carnot created a napkin holder down to the last detail, as well as an antique garment using his fantastic capacity to manufacture morphothosenes (at which he is a master). He mentally suggested the following:

"Greet that gentleman and offer him this souvenir to see what will happen."

Following his instructions, I went through the middle of the luxurious trees and inviting benches, stopping next to an elderly gentleman that appeared to be in his eighties. He had a long beard and did not appear at all friendly.

However, when he saw the napkin holder, engraved with a coat of arms, he smiled radiantly and embraced me, as he asked where I had gotten such a rare and precious jewel. Examining my garments, he identified the area and the time frame that I represented to him. He immediately familiarized me with the characters in his vivid recollections, referring to a count, a doctor and a baroness, as if he were living frozen in time, talking to himself, immersed in the details of a 19th century court. I did not get the feeling that I knew this extraphysical consciousness.

This event demonstrated once again that passing through the first death, or final projection, does not instantly transform one. We continue to behave as we did at the time when we discarded the soma. This condition continues until we have an inner transformation, which brings about changes in our opinions, introduces new ideas and allows the installation of the degree of self-control of all bodies that one is capable of.

The continuous spring-like climate in this extraphysical region, that surrounded this rest home, was conducive to the convalescence of extraphysical consciousnesses as they gradually recovered from their senile psychotic fantasies and the biological shock suffered resulting from the deactivation of their somas.

I thanked Carnot and left his recovery paradise. As I glided between trees and grassy patches, the unending concert was playing a lovely song performed by intangible instruments. The emotive composition resembled the Russian melodies of the Cossacks, as well as the songs and dances of glorious earth ballets.

Passing through one of the alleys in that natural hospital-park, I came upon huge patches of wild flowers that resembled a flower-planted mall I had seen in Washington. Within moments I was at the physical base.

After returning

The clock showed 10:11 p.m. I got up immediately to write down the recollections of all my perceptions and actions while in the projected state which, little by little were arriving in a fragmented fashion, still enveloped by the sounds of the oriental melody.

44. EXTRAPHYSICAL SLEEPWALKING

Prior to projection

Monday, November 26, 1979. Phase of the moon: first quarter at 6:09 p.m. I went to bed at 6:58 p.m. and laid down in the dorsal position. Ambient temperature, 73.5° F. Relative humidity 65%. It had been a rainy day. I was sleepy. Pulse: 58 bpm. No energy exercises were performed.

Extraphysical period

The helpers did not make themselves visible. They simply indicated that an extraphysical consciousness needed to be rescued immediately. I was perfectly lucid. The locale was near the apartment.

I saw a sleepwalking psychotic post-mortem, insistently mentally repeating that his name was Ago. He appeared to be some 68 years old. He had a large, oblong face and was wearing a huge jacket with chewing tobacco in the pockets. The whole ensemble reeked of tobacco smoke. I did what I could to awaken him and a helper soon took him away. I had the impression that this extraphysical consciousness had been Italian during his intraphysical life.

The helpers then brought an extremely beautiful, and very lethargic, 27-year-old blonde woman wearing an orange dress. It seemed that she had recently died in an accident, leaving her in a state of shock and immersed in an endless sleep.

As I woke her, she clung to my psychosoma the same way a child would upon meeting its father. Carrying her in my extraphysical arms, I left her in the care of a helper before returning to the soma.

The helpers had placed a calmly sleeping elderly male extraphysical consciousness next to my bed. After sending him a few long energy emissions and moving him farther from the bed, I felt an irresistible call to return to the soma. The psychosoma reentered the physical body in a sudden imposed return from above.

After returning

I immediately awoke with total lucidity. As I tried to recover my emotional balance, a helper arrived, performed brief energy emissions, transmitted a vigorous energetic flow and gave me some "audible" instructions that I perceived clairaudiently. He then moved himself farther away, together with the sleeping extraphysical consciousness who, up until that time, had remained in my bedroom. I clearly felt the residual energies from the previous lethargic extraphysical consciousness. I felt this unpleasant "hot" energy mostly in the areas of my arms and legs, from whence the largest flow of energy had emanated. The perceived heat of these energetic flows appeared to be due to the still dense psychosoma of that consciousness.

Checking my pulse, I verified it to be 50 bpm; 8 bpm less than it measured before the projection. My hands were extremely cold, but my extremities did not feel cold. After the projection, the clock showed 7:48 p.m. It was still in the middle of the period of human anguish.

Observations

We can see that projection allows a detailed first-hand investigation of extraphysical facts. It enables the analysis of intraphysical and extraphysical consciousnesses and events, which are more unpredictable each night. I had had a brief cleansing projection this night, but had not dealt directly with all of the intruders. This often happens during extraphysical assistance. The three extraphysical consciousnesses involved in this projection were ailing due to the lethargic state caused by the biological shock of passing through biological death. They had had neither negative nor positive intentions. They were simply in a neutral, amoral condition, immersed in their post-mortem condition, and unaware of what they were doing.

The psychotic post-mortems in this chapter's projection had been recruited early in the afternoon, when I had participated in a meeting of a non-religious service organization in Rio de Janeiro, where I ended up serving as extraphysical bait. The helper had been absolutely correct when he had made the following mental comment upon the exit of the third extraphysical consciousness:

"There is a lot to be done. For example, it is a pity that intrusion is still not well understood on Earth. Have you ever thought about the increases in efficiency that the great service organizations such as the LBA (*Legião de Boa Vontade*, or Legion of Good Will), Red Cross, Salvation Army, AA centers, emergency hot lines and others of that nature could realize by establishing extraphysical cleansing services in their work centers?"

That's the way it is. We are here on earth to learn how to control the human body, but we do not always accomplish this. Everything has its proper time and place.

I should make it clear that projection of the psychosoma is neither dangerous nor frightening, as is often claimed to be in fabrications made regarding psychic matters The incapacitated soma does not become possessed by wandering extraphysical consciousnesses who may want to force one to channel a message or suffer an intrusive assault.

The silver cord appears to have a security mechanism, such as a vibrational valve that operates during projections of the psychosoma. It automatically closes the psychic entrances of the inanimate soma upon takeoff, making it impenetrable. This prevents invasion by foreign or ailing consciousnesses for the duration of the projection.

Intrusion begins as a mental process before it manifests on a physical level. In order for the intruder to install itself in one's mind, it is necessary for the extraphysical consciousness to find a psychological and emotional predisposition in its victim. An empty brain cannot be directly influenced, just as an extraphysical consciousness cannot couple with someone's inanimate body. Under certain conditions, utilizing existing energies or psychic individuals, it is possible for an intruder to move non-living things, but no one can "live" through a rock, for example.

The silver cord is extremely powerful. It functions on a continuous basis. As a result, there is no closer connection than the one between the soma and the psychosoma during intraphysical life. The forces that circulate through the silver cord are the most powerful of the trio of the soma, silver cord and psychosoma. This is the case independent of any changes in the "bodies" and the aura.

The soma becomes vacant only when one passes through the first death – the final projection. This does not occur while the person is alive or during projections of the psychosoma. While one is projected, the "empty brain" condition is apparent, but the silver cord still occupies the soma in this case, like a powerful octopus protecting its territory.

45. INTERFERENCE FROM THE PAST

Prior to projection

Wednesday, November 28, 1979. At 4:50 in the afternoon, the extraphysical consciousness José Grosso advised me that I would definitely have a projection as soon as I laid down. At 6:04 p.m. I stretched out on the bed in the dorsal position, placing three pillows under my body. The ambient temperature was 77°F. Humidity: 60%. As I concentrated, I felt an invisible right hand on the forehead.

Extraphysical period

As I left the soma, I immediately awoke next to an extraphysical consciousness who informed me that we would go for an extraphysical spin right here in Rio de Janeiro.

Within moments, we left my apartment building and observed the goings-on in the street below. It was still light. For the first time, I became aware of several extraphysical consciousnesses riding in cars next to human drivers and passengers. I noticed this in a general manner, as well as specific cases in a gas station and in a "dune buggy" on the street in which a young couple was riding.

Some of the persons passing by were accompanied by one or more intimately connected extraphysical consciousness, seeming to be "composite persons". A young man under the impulsive influence of an extraphysical consciousness that was attached to him, was speaking loudly inside a convertible. It was quite astonishing to witness the cool, overt intrusion. It is incredible how persons can be influenced. It is impossible to grasp such a thing! It is much worse than I ever imagined. Intruders are truly energetic parasites. This reality is so incredible that, in order to fully appreciate it, one has to observe the interrelationships and the perfect juxtapositioning or coupling of the intraphysical and extraphysical consciousnesses. It is such a complete body-to-body coupling that it resembles the coexistence or alignment of one's own psychosoma and soma.

My expanded vision while outside of the soma allowed me to distinguish everything that was going on between the two consciousnesses that were "welded" together. The extraphysical consciousness was a middle-aged male preying on the unprotected mind of the young man who appeared to be some 25 years old. The youth was blond, strong, broad-shouldered and tanned. He was being "spoken through," expressing himself in loud yells and wild gestures, as he communicated with his friends who were in other convertibles with the tops down. To what extent were drugs an influencing factor in this case of intrusion? The helper did not interfere in this situation.

From there, we went on to other locations. Many details associated with this projection were lost from my memory, in whole or in part, as a result of my strong emotional reaction to witnessing the process of intrusion in its guileless plenitude.

I only remember that, later on, we entered a wide park where several people were sitting down resting, while others were walking their dogs.

The helper made various comments on how trees are a source of psychic energy to humans. He also addressed the necessity of maintaining positive thoughts while performing any task of great responsibility on Earth.

Next, my attention was captured by a sculpture in the middle of the park. Some extraphysical consciousnesses approached me and suggested:

"Try to remember and you will understand better. Try to remember!"

I looked upon the sculpture, trying to perform a reading of the piece. It was impossible to describe exactly what happened next. In the span of a few moments I perceived scenes involving this work of art. I suddenly felt myself involved in morphothosenes that caused an instantaneous and incontestable recapitulation of events. I recalled that I had been an obscure artist who had worked with the ornamentation of tombs in France centuries earlier.

As I changed my focus, the vision of the psychosoma had been substituted by the direct vision of the mentalsoma, and from human memory I shifted temporarily to integral memory.

The helper, noticing my stupefaction, realized that I had remembered something and mentally explained:

"During several of your recent projections, you have been tuning your thoughts to the wavelength of that particular existence in the distant past. This fixed idea has impacted your ability to operate freely. It has interfered in your deliberations and has sabotaged your projective recall. Observe closely and you will understand."

Still impressed by the brief vision, I remembered several target locations which I had projected to in this series of projections. Included in this recollection were three projections that I have previously described. They involve the tombstones in a cemetery (chapter 17), the observation of a high-relief decoration on an extraphysical gate (chapter 29), and the sculptures in an abandoned temple in the interior of Africa (chapter 31).

That explained it! The fragmentary recollection of those distant intraphysical lives has interfered in extraphysical tasks and explorations, as well as interfering with the performance of the projected psychosoma.

The helper further clarified:

"When temporarily liberated from physical matter, the freed consciousness has the capacity to immerse itself in the past and reengage the currents of forgotten experiences. The abilities developed in past intraphysical lives come to the surface of the integral memory and sometimes exhume an ancient man from within himself ..."

It was a great lesson in past-life recall. The extraphysical dimension is a thought-based world, where everything is dependent upon the nature and expression of thoughts in each circumstance and opportunity. The extraphysical consciousness is what it thinks. The powerful unconscious, full of past-life memories, often undermines the powers of recall of the projected consciousness through interference caused by ignored repressions.

I needed to recognize this fact with candor, leaving recollections of the past behind in peace, in order to allow me to accomplish things in 1979 – also in peace. I needed to seriously meditate on this issue. It explained my sculptures in the sand and the cases of what is commonly referred to in psychology as frustrated vocations. Logically, it becomes imperative to recall projections more readily, avoiding counterproductive self-suggestions and the loss of opportunities, even if the recollections are from one's own remote past.

I then saw a person listening to beautiful classical music at high volume on a small portable radio. We left the park and I returned to the soma with the music still resonating in my mind. I was fascinated by the melody as I entered my soma, because I could hear the rhythms expanding inside me. I was still engaged by the music, while more or less inside the soma in a cataleptic state, when an extraphysical consciousness touched the left leg in order to awaken me, so that I could register the extraphysical events.

After returning

I could still hear the melody as I opened my eyes. The extraphysical events came to me in their entirety, vivid, strong, and surprisingly natural, as soon as I began recalling them. Even so, as the psychosoma returned, many recollections were lost in the obscure corners of the mind.

The development of the ability to recall events experienced while outside the soma requires much practice and serenity, as well as good powers of observation. This last capacity is especially important for the accurate perception of extraphysical objects, personalities and occurrences in the extraphysical dimension.

The clock showed 7:24 p.m. As always, the position of the soma upon awakening was identical to that before takeoff. The soma was in the dorsal position wearing a v-neck pajama and without any blankets covering it.

Observations

I realize that the helper must have enhanced my extraphysical vision to allow me to coldly witness the intrusion of extraphysical consciousnesses upon humans in order to understand and cure them. Through the psychometry of the sculptured pieces and the prior life that was consequently recalled, I was able to better understand and resolve my personal case of naive but counterproductive self-obsession. I am sincerely grateful for their positive intentions.

46.   A COMPULSIVE REACTION

Prior to projection

Sunday, December 2, 1979. I laid in bed for my third sleep at 1:17 a.m., after having written for more than half-an-hour. Temperature: 77°F. Humidity: 62%. I assumed the classic dorsal position.

Extraphysical period

I had the sensation of being outside of the soma next to a huge house with many people inside. It appeared to be a gambling spot. There were numerous intraphysical and extraphysical consciousnesses. I was apparently alone and decided to leave the place in order to inspect the outside environment. A very well dressed gentleman was going down a stairway leading to the ocean. A lamppost illuminated the passage. Beside the lamppost, a man who looked like a policeman was gazing at the ocean in the distance. I followed a deserted path down between some trees. As I glided down the path, I came upon a suspicious-looking man hiding behind the trees. My immediate impulse was to run and hide somewhere in order not to be seen by the potential assailant. I left the path and was about to turn back, when I emembered that I was outside of the soma and, as such, had nothing to be afraid of. It was an intensely shocking realization.

I tried to understand the situation. The whole environment appeared to be so incredibly real! I regarded the suspicious-looking shabbily dressed young man. He was hiding in the shrubs and was armed with a gun. But, even if he could see me, he was certainly not able to shoot me.

I had reacted instinctively while in the psychosoma and started to laugh over my ridiculous fear and stupefaction from the conflicting impulses. The fact is that I was ashamed of my reaction. Laughter was simply an escape. I am in my "extraphysical childhood" but very much aware of it. I must maintain a presence of mind in all decisions that need to be made during a projection.I must search for and discover all my compulsive human habits similar to this one that I transfer to the projected consciousness in order to gradually eliminate them. I must have more discipline and training in order to leave the human body and obtain better and more useful results during these experiments. It is absolutely necessary to be properly prepared.

The psychosoma has all of the perceptive capacities of the soma, as well as its emotional reactions, including socially conditioned reflexes. To a certain extent, it even has the libido of the human personality.

I decided not to interfere with the man or his intentions. I simply sent him a positive, fraternal thought. I did not see any extraphysical consciousness next to him. I advanced a little and was able to see some men walking alone together in the hot twilight. One of them would more likely than not become a victim. Further down, a truck was parked in a backyard, in the middle of several trees. I circled the area to see if I could identify the place. It appeared that I was at the edge of Guanabara Bay in the north zone of Rio de Janeiro, not too far from the international airport. I felt the need to return home and back to the soma, which occurred within moments.

After returning

I woke up in the dorsal position in bed. My whole soma felt heavy and numb, and the joints made cracking noises when moved. As I turned onto the left side, the memory of everything that I had perceived and done while in the extraphysical dimension came to me in its entirety. I started to laugh at myself again over the fear I had had of being robbed. I still felt a little ashamed over my ridiculous behavior. Would it have been best to try to dissuade the thief from his intentions, or to try to warn those men of the imminent danger?

Observations

I recall that situations similar to the one related above have occurred in other projections. In chapter 14, a similar reaction provoked the automatic levitation of the psychosoma. Common observations made during everyday intraphysical life make their appearances in the extraphysical dimension. On one occasion, the sight of an extraphysical consciousness passing through a stone wall prompted me to go after it, to see if there were signs of a forced entry. This all transpired like a scene from a cartoon. The artificial social standards of human existence and our habitual patterns of thought in intraphysical life have profound effects on our reactions to events witnessed while in the extraphysical dimension. In the extraphysical environment, thinking, wishing, and acting occur simultaneously. Any incoherences on our part then manifest themselves immediately. I looked at the clock. It showed 2:26 a.m.

47. TEST PROJECTION

Prior to projection

Monday, December 3, 1979. Phase of the moon: full at 3:09 p.m. Ambient temperature: 72°F. Humidity: 51%. I laid in bed in the dorsal position.

I was in a good mood when I initiated energy emission exercises at 7:12 p.m. Within moments, the extraphysical consciousness José Grosso appeared and suggested that I leave the air conditioning on low. He also suggested that I not be concerned with the noise of the thunder or the lightning flashes. I was to perform a test projection in order to ascertain that all adverse physical circumstances can be overcome by the will-power of the projector. I first sat up in bed and performed several self-energizations to the head and solar plexus. Later, I did the same while in the dorsal position.

After a while, it started to rain. The flashes of lightning were so bright that I could perceive them through my eyelids.

The storm raged on as I began to experience some phenomena while still inside the body. I saw some brief visual images of an extraphysical friend of mine who was dressed like a doctor. I could feel slight partial separations of the extraphysical arms, and a swaying sensation due to the psychosoma moving from side to side. I could also hear the incessant thunder and the ever present noise of the air conditioner, which was situated close to the bedroom ceiling in alignment with the bed.

At one point, I experienced a slight repercussion as a result of a sudden return of the right extraphysical leg that had been in partial non-alignment with the soma. The soma was numb and the psychosoma was partially projected and partially in alignment. I felt pressure at the base of the skull and then experienced a smooth, upwards takeoff.

Extraphysical period

I left the bedroom and was aware of gliding in the living room. My thoughts were fixed on the idea of the experiment at hand. I looked for my wife and, strangely, she was not there. I saw the clock's swaying pendulum, examined a shelf with ornamental dishes and vases, and closely observed the numbers 376-500 in a location that I was not able to record in my memory. Afterwards, I left the apartment through the living room window and found myself in the middle of a raging thunderstorm. I felt nothing abnormal or unusual; not even the raindrops or the lightning. I was flying in complete serenity high above the traffic, when I received an inner warning to return to the base. I did so immediately.

After returning

I opened the eyelids without experiencing any lapse in awareness. As usual, the perception of time had been unclear but I had the impression that the projection had lasted only a few minutes. The soma remained numb, cold, and in the dorsal position. The storm had abated slightly. My memory remained intact but I was intrigued by two things. Where was my wife? What were the numbers that I had seen?

The clock showed 8:53 p.m. As I opened the bedroom door and was about to step into the hallway, my wife came in from the living room. I asked her where she had been, since she was normally in the living room at that time of night and I had not found her there. She explained that she had gone to the garage to find a better parking spot for the car. We looked for the numbers that I had examined but had, so far, not been able to locate. After some time, my wife recalled what the numbers were. They were the serial number of a set of magazines with sequential numbering from 376 to 500. They were part of a collection that had been glued together and stored in one of the living room shelves, situated at a height of 9 feet. In order to read the sticker, one would have to climb up on a chair or step ladder. The consciousness, while in the psychosoma, has no problem overcoming the physical restrictions of height and distance.

Observations

I systematically registered all the occurrences, satisfied with the complete success of the brief projective experience that the helper had sponsored. With his assistance, I had been able to project myself in spite of the noise from the air conditioning, the claps of thunder, and the flashes of lightning from the raging storm. This was the first time in my existence that I had projected under those conditions.

This experience offered new material for study and experimentation which could yield a new interpretation of the phenomenon of projection. The projector's will-power, forceful desire, perseverance and patience, coupled with vigorous mental capacities, are capable of overcoming all apparent physical obstacles to projection.

After projecting during a storm, it became apparent that we are projectively capable of anything. The mental capacities and habits of the projector are more important than his or her physical surroundings. On the other hand, the projector is decidedly an experimenter or explorer. The joining of these conditions is inevitable, given that a greater knowledge and interest on the projector's part serve to enhance projective results.

The most effective technique allowing an exchange with extraphysical consciousnesses that the helpers have used with me is the process they call psychophonic (channeled) monologue. In this process, they are coupled with me and speak *to* me by talking *through* me, using my vocal apparatus, while I am physically alone in the bedroom. During these periods, I remain entirely lucid and semi-projected, slightly above and to the rear of the soma.

In this fashion, when I think of a question, the extraphysical consciousness responds immediately, speaking audibly through my own vocal mechanism. This system allows the recording of information and has proven to be the most efficient of all, being far more reliable than automatic writing or clairaudience. This capacity, when well developed, offers a cleaner transmission of information without interference and "psychic static." It is less demanding than automatic writing and is more authentic for the contemporary psychic. It is also faster and more dynamic.

This process should only be practiced by the veteran psychic, when alone and with trustworthy extraphysical assistance in an adequate environment, in order to avoid negative interferences from either dimension. Psychophonic (channeled) monologue, because of its simplicity and efficiency, is perhaps the most advanced human conquest in the area of psychic technology in this century, aside from the codification of spiritism. Anyone who doubts this has only to experiment for themselves. It is, without a doubt, the best psychic accessory to the projection of the psychosoma.

---

48. THE MIRROR AND TIME

Prior to projection

Friday, December 7, 1979. Some energy exercises were performed at 7:12 p.m. The temperature in the bedroom was 79°F. Humidity: 57%. I laid down in the dorsal position. I was in a good mood and was thinking about having a projection.

Extraphysical period

I could not determine where the sleep state ended and projection began. I found myself projected next to a longtime extraphysical acquaintance, who I owe much and have given the name of Transmentor. This extraphysical consciousness knows everything about me in this intraphysical life and many others. I have extraphysical friends who I have not seen for a long time for various reasons, ranging from undertaking new tasks in other areas, preparing themselves for a new intraphysical life, or going on long trips to other populated planets, that are spread throughout the universe. This friend, however, has made himself present over a long span of time, in all kinds of circumstances.

We arrived at a house in the physical dimension and Transmentor made himself invisible. The simple residence had a small garden separated from the street by a fence. A two-year-old child was playing in the garden with a three-year-old. The smaller of the two children had soiled its clothes while playing and, as the older one tried to clean them, appeared to see me. I spoke calmly to both children and told them to go into the house and look for their mother. At that point, a ten-year-old child appeared and all four of us went in the house into a kind of dining area where the children's mother sat with a tray in her lap.

The three-year-old told her mother that she had seen a man and had heard him talk, but they all playfully dismissed the subject. As I left the dining area and entered a small room, I passed in front of a mirror and a curious thing happened. I saw my image reflected in the mirror but only the head, the shoulders and a portion of the chest. It was indeed my face, but taller, better looking and with my bald head even shinier. There was no question that my overall size had increased. Observing the image as objectively as possible, I was intrigued. What was I seeing there? Was it that my psychosoma was denser than usual, carrying a larger portion of the holo-chakra? How could I see my image if I was able to see through the mirror and even through the wall? Was that why the child was able to see me? Or was this image a morpho-thosene?

The issue before me and my innate curiosity left me in a state of total confusion. Although I tried to control my emotions, I soon felt a clear signal telling me to return to the soma. As in other projections, the powerful emotional reaction brought an abrupt end to the projection.

After returning

I opened the eyes, stretched the entire soma to relieve its stiffness and looked at the clock. It was 8:43 p.m. The recollections came to me in whole, and with them, the confusion caused by the event with the mirror. I was lying in bed, thinking about the matter, when Transmentor arrived and explained that I had actually seen myself that way because the psychosoma had been denser than usual while projected. This shows that a greater density of the psychosoma does not affect the expanded extraphysical vision of the lucid projector.

I realized that the projection had lasted almost an hour. This leads me to conclude that the events took place at a slower rate than they would have in intraphysical life, as the psychosoma was denser than usual and was projected on the planet's crust. The slower development of events had allowed me to recall them in their entirety.

Observations

The factor of time influences the projector's ability to recall events. Time, as we understand it, does not exist for the psychosoma – only for the soma. The psychosoma contains a minute amount of subtle matter and coordinates the functions of the soma. We always use our psychosoma and, in fact, live in it.

We can thus conclude that the psychosoma suffers a slight influence of time during a projection, especially in events directly related to the takeoff from and the return to the soma. Also, when the psychosoma is projected in the intraphysical dimension, it is denser and suffers an indirect influence of time. When the psychosoma is in a pure extraphysical dimension, devoid of constant morphothosenes, the projector frees himself a little more each time from the density of the intraphysical dimension and the influence of time. Thus, we can also conclude that the faster extraphysical events occur, the more difficult it becomes for the projector to transfer recall of those events from projected consciousness to the memory bank of the physical brain or, in other words, recall the events experienced. This is due to velocity and the non-existence of relative time.

49. MENTAL BALANCE

Prior to projection

Saturday December 8, 1979. Second sleep, lying on the right side. Temperature in the bedroom: 79°F. Humidity: 57%. The time was 12:26 a.m..

Extraphysical period

I recall being led by a helper to an extraphysical region. Here, I was shown the processes of intrusion on Earth. In other words, the mental war between the extraphysical and the intraphysical dimension, and the consequent effort that those working with tasks having to do with evolution need to make in order to master their own thoughts. The processes used by minds that are clouded by insanity are unimaginable and unbelievable.

In order not to disseminate the undignified side of the facts or produce excessive negative inspirations similar to those sponsored by the media, the helper recommended that I summarize the extraphysical facts witnessed without making counterproductive suggestions to unbalanced minds.

I noticed various examples of negative forces undermining edifying work. One was the construction of a dike in the wrong spot. Instead of containing influxes from seaquakes, it actually helped the violent waters to move inland and destroy everything in their path. Another example was that of a small child who became hydrophobic and attacked its mother, unwittingly transmitting the rabies virus.

Several clandestine criminal organizations operate in human society. They work outside of the law in an atmosphere of camouflaged terror. This climate of intense mental sadism and parasitism is a result of associations made with shady extraphysical consciousnesses having extraordinary magnetic powers. This illustrates the evolutionary level of adversities which the Earth has been going through in the last millenniums.

Finally, I was privy to the outright intrusive manipulation of a human scientist working with full awareness and conviction on malignant objectives ranging from genocide and mass insanity, to bacteriological war and even the neutron bomb. This was occurring at great human and financial expense, with government approval.

Fortunately, it is impossible to create an extraphysical psychic virus that attacks the psychosoma, although in the shadowy zones of the extraphysical dimension it has been attempted countless times. We must recognize that, either here or there, sooner or later, but definitely at the "right time," the consciousness is always reborn into continuing evolution, and one's unbalances can be overcome. This allows for the resurgence of peace and consciential growth. The universal balance directs even the transitory disturbances that occur during the advancement of evolution. It all remains under immutable control. After these events, I was accompanied to the physical base in order to awaken.

After returning

The clock showed 1:53 a.m. An avalanche of extraphysical images from the projection came to me with incredible clarity and vigor.

Observations

The helpers suggested that I provide the reader with my medical profile: age, 47; height, 5'6.5"; weight, 159 lbs.; electrocardiogram and electroencephalogram, both normal; heart rate, 58 beats per minute. I have never been treated or even examined by a psychiatrist, parapsychologist, psychologist, psychoanalyst, or priest. I have never needed to attended gatherings for the treatment of intrusion, and have never undergone hypnosis. Thirteen of my teeth have fillings, in case this fact has any relevance. Two medications, P.40 and S.25 (initials only), are currently used in the routine treatment of hypertension, a "close friend" of mine since the age of 28. Such drugs are dangerous and should only be taken under medical prescription. Even then, all possible precautions should be taken.

P.40 cannot be prescribed to all patients suffering from hypertension, only to a few cases. A technical explanation of its effects follows: the sympathetic nervous activity is mediated by two different types of receptors, classified as beta and alpha. The stimulus produced by the sympathomimetic amino acids are mediated entirely by the beta-adrenergic receptors and P.40 blocks the beta-adrenergic receptors. In other words, it prevents excessive stimulus of the catecholimines in the heart, where beta receptors exist. The blocking of the sympathetic stimulus causes a reduction in the heart rate (chronotropic effect) as well as the strength of the contraction of the myocardium (inotropic effect). The reduction of the heart rate increases the predisposition of the soma to allow the projection of the psychosoma.

S.25 is a vascular anti-spasmogenic. It is used in the prevention and treatment of disturbances of the central circulatory system by inhibiting vaso-active spasmogenic substances capable of constrictive activities such as serotonin, adrenaline, noradrenaline, angiotensin, vasopressin, dopamine and bradykinin. This medication promotes the central arteriovenous micro-circulation, which allows a greater blood flow to the tissues. This alleviates disturbances of the cerebral circulation and prevents the dependent symptoms of involuntary arteriosclerotic processes such as lack of concentration, memory loss, sleep disturbances and mental fatigue. When used intermittently, it effectively promotes the projection of the psychosoma as well as projective recall.

I use these medications as a result of my hypertension. There are many catalytic agents capable of promoting the projection of the psychosoma, aside from drugs. I do not, however, recommend them. In fact, the only one I endorse is the ironclad will of the projector, which by far is one of the most powerful and safe projective agents that exist.

50. BREATHING AND TAKEOFF

Prior to projection

Sunday, December, 9, 1979. I went to bed at 7:23 p.m. I had spent the entire afternoon typing this book. As I laid in the dorsal position with the arms and legs stretched out, no energy exercises took place. The air conditioning was switched on in my office and the adjoining door to the bedroom was kept open. The temperature was 81°F. Relative air humidity was 54%. It had been very hot during the day, the temperature having reached 101°F. I was tranquil, as I happily concentrated on the idea of ceasing to feel the soma and floating above it. I was certain that something would happen.

Extraphysical period

The soma became numb. As I remained completely immobile, I experienced total lucidity and heightened reasoning capacities. I soon stopped feeling the feet, legs, hands, arms, abdomen and trunk in that exact order. It was at that point that I began to observe myself. It was as though I was living solely inside of my cranium, with great lucidity. The neck and face actually ceased to serve as intraphysical sensorial references. My mental activity continued to be extraordinarily rational and serene. I received mental suggestions to induce the experiences and verify the physiological sensations that accompany a projection, throughout the process.

I started to notice not the emission of energy, but the slow takeoff of the psychosoma from the soma. There appeared to be a rhythm to the emission of the psychosoma. The process was not transpiring in its entirety, but rather, as if segments of the psychosoma were "bubbling up" little by little and floating some 8 to 12 inches above the body. I kept feeling the impressions of the oscillating rhythm of the psychosoma that started inside the soma at the source of the whole process. With the eyes closed, I could hear several sounds. I could hear the distant air conditioning and the yells of children in a neighboring playground. A few minutes later, my wife and son came into the hallway. My wife proceeded to close the bedroom door, which muffled the sound of the air conditioning. I could hear them whispering. I wasn't awakened by any particular noise, because I had not gone to sleep.

The *super-mind* of the psychosoma was still trapped inside the physical head, but the rest of the psychosoma was more out than in. The condition felt pleasant. Although my eyes were shut, I was enjoying greater lucidity than that experienced during the waking state. I clearly felt that life had been multiplied many times, and was certain of being partially inside the white and gray matter of the brain, but portions of the consciousness had already passed beyond the gray matter. Consciousness was expanding beyond the cranium.

I was advised to leave the physical head by rolling the psychosoma to the left and to observe as closely as possible all the sensations involved, in order to report them later. With that invisible assistance, and under my conscious and voluntary control, the light psychosoma, in a condition of low density, projected outwards and to the side, by rolling to the left and then to the right. I provoked various separations and returns by rolling first to one side and then to the other.

I felt that the sensation of breathing is, without a doubt, the most intense physical sensation. It is also the last one to be lost upon leaving the soma and the first one that is regained upon returning. It is much more impressive than circulation or the heartbeat. Breathing is the most vibrant sensation involved in the projective process.

This fact confirms the value of yoga exercises, which allow a person to hold and control the breath, the flow of blood, and even to slow down the heart rate through deep concentration. In this way, one can significantly aid the projection of the psychosoma. In summary: conscious projection techniques are, above all, mental, although rhythmic breathing helps. I never practiced yoga and I do not perform rhythmic breathing. However, experience shows that there exists a strong correlation between the processes. That is perhaps the reason why Orientals who practice breathing exercises have a high projection rate.

Breathing is a heavy, crude process compared to those of the subtle psychosoma. Once, when I was completely outside the soma, I was no longer breathing and thought about regaining the process. In that same instant, I started to breathe and immediately returned to the soma. This is also a characteristic of the near-death experience, so extensively studied recently.

During this period of the trance of consecutive projections, respiration while in the soma remained steady. What varied were the sensations of breathing or the repercussions experienced by the psychosoma. The sensation of the breath stopping is incredibly pleasant. In intraphysical life, although it may not seem to be so, the natural process of breathing is a heavy load that mankind carries constantly. In my judgment, the loss of breathing is what begins to establish the sense of lightness of the psychosoma, the subsequent euphoria during takeoff, constitutes the fundamental condition for extraphysical levitation, and the freeing of the psychosoma from the strong pull of the silver cord, thus predisposing it to free flight.

Everything that I have described about the successive projective takeoffs happened within a radius of 13 feet of the influence of the powerful energetic cord around the dense body. This gives credibility to the idea that the psychosoma loses the sensation of breathing while still inside this area of actuation of the silver cord, although it is the silver cord that makes respiration and circulation possible. That is why it is necessary to know how to control the psychosoma, in order to administrate projections.

A projector during a projection, as well as yogis, ascetics, xamans, fakirs, lamas, Zulu witches, exorcists and mediums, when they enter into a trance, possess many points in common. The most salient is the physiological phenomenon of breathing. If, during a projection, the projector thinks about breathing, he will. Depending on the circumstances, this may cause an immediate return of the psychosoma – especially if it is projected close to the soma.

The psychosoma does not need to breathe. Breathing is the principal process through which only the material mass of the soma is fed. I experimented several times by quickly switching between takeoff and return, from euphoria to heaviness to euphoria, etc. It is comparable to a balance scale with unequal weights in its dishes. The euphoria of being in the psychosoma is represented by one dish, with its inexpressibly extraordinary sensation of expansion. The heaviness of the soma, the heavy apparatus that carries the psychosoma, is represented by the other dish. It is as if the consciousness swings from one plate to the other under the command and determination of the will.

That is why, with time, the projector can easily determine when they are dreaming and when they are projected, in very much the same way that he or she recognizes the difference between being asleep and awake. This is because projection is a continuation of the waking state, except that one can experience a profound expansion of the consciousness. If troubled individuals were able to have even a single projection similar to the ones that occurred this night, the world would be completely different! How many mistakes would be avoided! How many destinies would change for the better!

Whoever has even a single truly lucid projection, even if projected close to the soma, will be entirely convinced of having left the material body, in spite of opinions to the contrary. This is because projection provides irrefutable evidence of the survival of biological death, to the point that it becomes absurd, foolish and annoying to discuss it. It is worth mentioning that obtaining one's first projection, with at least 50% of extraphysical lucidity, forever marks the psyche, inevitably generating changes in the projector's way of life. The experience constitutes a decisive and transcendental personal achievement that causes one to change personal habits and transform one's general living conditions, social and religious activities, and even sleeping and eating habits.

On a night such as this, when conditions are exceptionally favorable, everything seems to occur easily, without incident, spontaneously and naturally within the parameters of projection. I did not even notice the magnetic pull of the silver cord. Could this have been a more favorable day due to the status of my psychophysical biorhythms?

There are other nights, when everything is difficult and strenuous, and obstacles appear unexpectedly. Very often, it is simply impossible to provoke a projection, however one desires and insists upon it. On the other hand, there are countless known factors that affect projection and possibly as many unknown factors that we ignore. It is necessary to learn more in order to have projections on a regular basis.

Ideal projections are very much like the ones I had today, because they do not include intervals of unconsciousness, periods of sleep, dreaming, coma or even awakening. They are not induced through pain, thirst, fear, fasting, exhaustion, drugs, emotional stress, hypnosis or any other techniques, systems, approaches, methods or artificial means. A takeoff and return and another take-off and return of the consciousness from and to the soma occurred in a consecutive manner. They were smooth and happened according to the interdependent physiological processes of the two bodies, which are inherent in human nature.

Thus, projection is a common physiological activity, attainable by everyone with a sound mind. The basic foundations of projection are strengthened and expanded through frequent psychophysical exercises, in other words, mental and physical relaxation.

I was only able to obtain extraphysical visual clarity during one of the takeoffs of the psychosoma. As soon as I began returning to the soma, the extraphysical vision would immediately begin to darken again. This shows that the extraphysical vision also begins within the perimeter of influence of the silver cord, or nearer the soma.

As I now started rolling the psychosoma to the side, its adherence to the soma would weaken and the strength of breathing would diminish. At that point, I was not even able to hear the heartbeats. As the psychosoma completed one full rotation, breathing disappeared. I left the soma and returned to it, rolling to the right and then to the left, four times, in slow motion. I carefully observed the sensations of the process in every detail. The takeoff of the psychosoma has its own rhythm. It is like a ballet, a pleasant ballet.

The soma is a powerful and heavy machine. A soma weighing 154 pounds appears to be a lot heavier than it really is in comparison to the lightness of the psychosoma, which is observed to be about one thousandth of the body weight – in this case 2.5 ounces. Comparatively speaking, it is as though the projected psychosoma were a grain of rice and the soma a ton of granite, into which the grain of rice enters and takes control during the "landing" process.

I also noticed that the psychosoma appears to be somewhat shrunken while outside the soma. When re-entering the body, it seems to increase in volume and weight like a balloon that, when filled inside of a mold, assumes the form of the human body. The psychosoma is ant-like in comparison to the elephant-like soma.

While outside the soma with the emotions under perfect control, I stood up twice inside the expanded bedroom. Next, I laid the psychosoma down again in order to closely observe the sensations of lucid takeoff. I would like to stress again that this is the most important and impressive stage of the projection process.

Each projection has its own peculiar characteristics. The clarity of the extraphysical experience is proportional to the projector's level of lucidity during the projection. The extraphysical sphere of energy is evidently always the same. What changes is the perceptive capacity of the consciousness.

After returning

During the various takeoffs and re-entries, I did not move any part of the soma. It remained numb the whole time, from 7:23 p.m. until 9:08 p.m., when I finally looked at the clock.

I did not awaken per se, because I maintained awareness throughout the process. I simply opened my eyelids and broke the numbness of the body. This had occurred a few times in this series of projections when my awakening corresponded to the simple opening of the eyelids and the natural suspension of the projective trance.

It was also not necessary to recall the extraphysical events, because all the facts were so vivid in my mind, just like the events that had transpired throughout the day. The only difference was that the extraphysical experiments were indelibly etched in my memory for two reasons: I had been in a state of *super consciousness*, and my attention had remained firmly focused on the progression of the phenomena.

Observations

I am living proof that the healthy provocation of projections of the psychosoma completely dispenses with all mysticism and rituals. Projection demands only the discipline of one's mental life and personal conduct, as does any other procedure that aims to improve one's physiological performance. Projection, therefore, is a natural physiological process. It is a human attribute inherent to one's life, as are sleep and psychic capacities or, if you wish, gymnastics, sports, eating, etc. The projector is a kind of "transcendent athlete."

Each projector gradually develops his or her own style or personal technique of projecting, according to his or her potential and lifestyle. The personal factors that most affect the quality of a projection are one's inner state, the natural process of projection, one's consciential status and the psychic faculties of the individual. I believe that developed psychic capacities help various aspects, principally in the amplification of the extraphysical perceptions.

51. PLANKS OF FLIGHT

Prior to projection

Tuesday, December 11, 1979. Phase of the moon: last quarter at 11:00 a.m. Third sleep at 1:09 a.m. in the dorsal position, after having written for some time in the office. Ambient temperature: 79°F. Humidity: 58%.

This evening's events were many and varied. Consequently, I used a memory system. I had quickly tagged the episodes in chronological order with key words. I had noted 19 scenes, relevant points, or different instances. I will now attempt to describe them in detail.

Extraphysical period

I awoke next to an extraphysical consciousness who explained that I was about to make an exploratory visit, acting as a human reporter, to an ancient extraphysical transition colony. This colony was located in the extraphysical region over Brazil.

The helpers spurred me into action, explaining that I was carrying a high coefficient of powerful energies that would act as a protective shield. During the distant and prolonged excursion, I should endeavor to remain serene at all times, taking in the occurrences calmly, with the certainty that, being a projected person, I would need above all to protect my life in this dimension. I should not allow myself to be affected by incessant advances and I could use the emission of energies defensively if necessary.

I should be as forthright as possible and should not under any circumstances hide my status as a projected person. I should retain the key element of each situation in order to help me recall it later. I should not lose sight of the fact that I am an adult, extraphysically speaking, and should act accordingly. I was advised to keep in mind that actions are instantaneous in the extraphysical dimension because they are directly generated by thoughts, not requiring physical actions.

I would be alone and observed from a distance, but would not receive any direct assistance or interference. I would have to rely on my own resources. I should be confident of succeeding.

After finishing the quick, succinct briefing, the helper examined me one last time and, as if sending a candidate off to undergo a test, he said:

"The density of your psychosoma will be determined by your thoughts and your will to absorb the "substances" that predominate in each environment. Remember to behave as though you were an extraphysical consciousness, but make clear your condition as a projected person. Maintain inner peace. Good luck."

We immediately set out flying through space and within moments I was left in a gloomy and poorly lit spot.

I came upon the edge of an enormous, deep pit full of rocks. It reminded me of a gorge or canyon, the kind you see in western movies. The only difference was the filth and the sewage-like water, some of which flowed slowly, but most of which was stagnating in deep puddles. I observed many extraphysical consciousnesses (an extraphysical society), gathered in groups on the edges. There were more on the side of the gorge that I was on.

I knew that the canyon was used for energetic defense by the colony, besides being a sewage system for the control of energetic pollution. The gorge was tortuous and was alternately deep and shallow.

I was looking for a way to cross over to the other side when, upon passing me, two tranquil male extraphysical consciousnesses hurriedly recommended that I move along, as this was no place for human beings. I was, therefore, easily recognizable as a projected person.

I began to walk around the edge of the canyon. Other extraphysical consciousnesses passed by. Some disfigured ones looked in my direction. One came running after me and yelled as if trying to frighten me:

"Get out! You can't stay here."

I arrived at the outskirts of a city that was next to the canyon, which snaked its way through the surrounding landscape.

I came upon a kind of vibrational dock. It seemed like the waves of morphothosenes in the crustal dimension had plunged forth and battered the gigantic dock structure. One could see an "ocean" of heavy elements and substances as far as the eye could see. This ocean resulted from the emissions of chronically diseased minds.

A faint yellowish light permeated the whole city. It seemed like the scenery was permanently immersed in an eternal gloom. I was not able to locate any planets or stars in the grayish sky.

As they passed me, a group of friendly-looking extraphysical consciousnesses warned:

"Beware of robbers."

Within moments a consciousness having a human form with animal-like features, incapable of hiding the evil, dark nature of its psychosoma, lunged at me with all of its might in a sudden extraphysical attack. It was frenetically trying to drain all the life force from me like a vampire or energetic leach. It seemed as though it would have inhaled me whole, if it could.

I tried to free myself from it by emitting energy of peace with all my might. Surprisingly, the extraphysical consciousness backed away as if it had received an electric shock, and disappeared as quickly as it had appeared.

It was impossible to hide my thoughts comparing the extraphysical mugger to its human counterparts. The negative intentions were the same. What differed was the objective of the attack. Could it be that intraphysical assailants end up like this one when they pass over to the extraphysical dimension?

I decided to leave that spot, but stayed on the same side of the canyon in order to explore the environment further. I was in a good mood and possessed incredible decision-making capacities. I felt the psychosoma to be unrestrained and balanced.

The pathway led upwards and I decided to follow it, walking like everyone else.

A horrid-looking elderly female extraphysical consciousness with sensual intentions exuberantly approached me in yet another extraphysical attack. Due to the repulsion that she inspired in me with her appearance and unrestrained emotions, I felt nothing but repugnance and disgust towards her. As I tried to rid myself of her, several young extraphysical consciousnesses looked on and laughed openly at my troubles. I knew that it would be useless to try to enlighten this extraphysical consciousness, as she was deeply set in her ways and her imbalances were already quite crystallized. In the extraphysical dimension nothing can be hidden. Our opposing sentiments were obvious and impossible to disguise.

After ridding myself of the demented extraphysical female, I decided to cross to the other side of the canyon through a narrow entrance that appeared to be semi-deserted. There were powerful positive energies in the immediate area. I walked on a little and found a park full of people gathered in groups. It was strange that the environment had improved but the appearances of the extraphysical consciousnesses had changed very little.

I carefully approached a pleasant average-looking male extraphysical consciousness. He had the kind of personality that made you feel certain that you had met him somewhere before. His psychosoma appeared to emit some light. I asked him what kind of place this was.

The mental response came like an echo, as if it had been yelled:

"Does it matter? There are hundreds of places equal to this one."

He smiled broadly, turned and left, leaving me standing there. Exchanges with extraphysical consciousnesses are not always polite. No one is capable of hiding their thoughts and sentiments, which are always apparent in one's own energetic psychosphere (aura).

I wanted to look for another projected person, as I thought it would be interesting to find a colleague in action. I left the area, inquiring where I might find one. I reasoned that there should be some, as these surroundings appeared to have strong ties with the Earth.

I circulated among the various groups for a while. Many I asked just shook their heads in a negative response to my query. Others would simply glance at me. The majority remained indifferent to my curiosity.

A male passer-by made a joke and laughed, provoking the laughter of many around him:

"I am made of flesh and bones! At least I wish I was..."

The humor implied that the extraphysical consciousness wanted a new intraphysical life. However, this option may not always be available to the inhabitants of that dimension.

Eventually, a young woman took me by the arm and declared with conviction:

"I will introduce you to someone human!"

In an instant, still inside the park, she took me to a 14-year-old female, dressed in red, completely deformed, seemingly blind, with an enormous head altered by hydrocephalus. Her red hair was neatly combed and parted down the middle. She was surrounded by three extraphysical consciousnesses.

I tried to approach her and sensed, even before asking, that she was projected while her body slept. To confirm this, I mentally questioned her and, without even moving her semi-open eyelids, framed by deformed eye sockets, she answered:

"Yes, I am from Earth."

She playfully retorted as the group exchanged looks and smiles:

"We are companions, friends, brothers..."

I also started to laugh when I identified the verse of the spiritist melody "Song of Christian Happiness" that they had been singing. I wanted to know more: where she had come from, and what she was doing there, but she cut me short and simply explained:

"I am a patient at a home for special children but I don't have any clout. There, I am half-dead..."

I understood immediately. Her condition, when back in the physical body, which was not apparent at that time, is even worse than when she is projected. Here, she is enjoying some precious moments of freedom with her friends.

After thanking her, I bid her and her friends farewell and left the park.

I entered a street with paved sidewalks, similar to those on Earth.

Did that street have any traffic? I could not see any.

I approached two male extraphysical consciousnesses. However, when I neared them, I realized that they were too deeply absorbed in their own intimate worlds, and gave up trying to communicate. They were obviously psychotic post-mortems, which made up a fair portion of the colony.

As I reached an open square, I witnessed a shocking and bizarre spectacle. I saw a large crowd of people united in a single mass and moving in wave-like motions as if they were dancing. They appeared to be satisfying one another with hugs and kisses in a most natural fashion. It appeared to be a group exchange of energy or a donation of vibrations by way of transfusions through direct contact – all done with a promiscuity of extremely bad taste. It gave the impression of an orgy.

The whole scene had a definite sexual connotation, devoid of malice. It was all being performed very naturally. How can we understand it, given the social structure on Earth, as well as current, human prejudice?

How can we pass judgment on practices that transcend the boundaries of our habits and behaviors? Was this cosmoethically correct conduct in that extraphysical region? Something there reminded me of scenes from contemporary alternative theater.

I left the humanoid waves circulating through the square and entered an alley with plain, unadorned houses on both sides. It was similar to the outskirts of cities found in the interior of Brazil. This environment was cleaner than any of the others. I was not sure what made the other environment dirty, but I could feel and see its dirt and grime.

I saw gentle hills and many buildings with rounded curves where there should have been sharp corners at the intersection of side streets. It was odd. This was the first time that I had seen streets separating city blocks without corners! All the blocks were rounded, and had no right angles.

The bluish-purple color of the majority of the houses was indelibly engraved in my memory. Many of the houses were attached to each other. Some had flower gardens. The colors were not ugly but rather picturesque; I do not recall any place on Earth or any human environment painted with such original and unique colors.

The buildings appeared to be as solid as physical ones. Sometimes, family dwellings, when observed while outside of the soma, can be seen through, as though they are transparent. Curiously, the houses in that alley were all opaque and impossible to see through. I also felt that I would not be able to pass through the walls of those residences as they were strangely solid.

The problem of density while in the extraphysical dimension is a serious one. The power of the mind to manifest its thoughts is shocking. The influence of the consciousness in forming its own environment occurs in any sphere of life. With that power, the mind is capable of obtaining impressive results.

In one of the streets, some of the extraphysical consciousnesses passing by approached me as if waiting to calmly embrace me for the purpose of receiving energies. They were obviously in lack. My only recourse was to extend my arms and to think firmly about emitting energies, energizing them without touching them.

I did this with four groups of two or three extraphysical consciousnesses. They knew that any projected person could give them the strength they needed in those circumstances.

Further down, I examined a public area with stands that looked as though they were made from concrete. I immediately understood that the extraphysical consciousnesses were gathering there in order to jointly improve and harmonize their thoughts. They appeared to be convalescing from the liberating process of their biological death. While many concentrated, others simply reflected. Still others blankly gazed straight ahead as if not seeing anything.

Next to the stands, I noticed a kind of gymnasium with huge metal structures that slightly resembled scaffolding, except that they were extremely high. I was going to ask someone what it was used for when I realized, after closer examination, that the extraphysical consciousnesses were climbing up the inside of the structure in order to practice flying. They would climb up the inside of the scaffolds with the strength of their thoughts and would rest on the crossbars whenever they felt tired.

The locale did not have the best environment for flight. Before leaving the site, I wanted to explore possibilities and try flying myself. In spite of mustering every bit of will-power, I could only fly at low altitude inside the scaffolding. Was it the density of the atmosphere that kept the psychosoma from flying? If so, there was a strong gravitational influence within the extraphysical colony. How would this extraphysical transitional area be rated on an evolutionary scale?

I then thought of returning to the physical base, thinking about the long string of events, the sequence of the facts that I had witnessed and the effort that I would have to make to recall everything and register it. I feel I have been able to portray the main events that occurred in that extraphysical colony. It is incredible how one can live and act outside of the soma in the infinite, unknown and transcendent multidimensional realms.

After returning

I woke up in the dorsal position. The clock showed 3:26 a.m. The extraphysical events came to me with an incredible clarity. I got up and wrote them down.

Observations

Some of the factors which most impede the recall of extraphysical events include: incorrect observations made by the projector; the numerous locations visited; maintenance of the psychosoma's stability while in transit; the recuperation of defects in the soma while projected; the transfer of information to the physical brain; and the impact of the psychosoma's return upon the physical brain. Aside from these factors, it is important to have good cortical circulation.

Extraphysical events are best remembered by the projector who enjoys extraphysical activities and truly wishes to recall them, by implementing deep self-analysis and overcoming the lapses in lucidity with an iron-clad will. There is no other solution. The differences between the human brain and the consciousness when projected, the intraphysical and extraphysical dimensions, the social conditioning of the human mind and the expansion of the projected consciousness are huge, intense and permanent. Many thousands of individuals have projections but are not aware, as they may be lucid while in the extraphysical dimension, but are not capable of recalling the extraphysical events that they have witnessed and even participated in.

52. FROZEN ATMOSPHERE

Prior to projection

Thursday, December 13, 1979. The last time I had looked at the clock, it had been a few minutes after 1:00 a.m. Position in bed: lying on the left side. Temperature: 79°F. Air humidity: 52%. Indirect air conditioning.

Extraphysical period

I found myself fully aware, beside an unknown extraphysical consciousness, who I greeted. This consciousness revealed that we would go to an unusual place within the intraphysical dimension.

I left Rio de Janeiro. The high speed flight only allowed an indefinite and confused perception of the area traveled.

Since thought and action are the same in the extraphysical dimension, we were soon flying over a frozen area. There was ice everywhere under the dark, starless night. The only light that could be seen was the soft, natural extraphysical illumination that can be seen wherever one is projected.

I wanted to look at myself, and noticed that I was wearing my customary projecting uniform – a blue, v-neck pajama – in the middle of the endless galleries.

In some areas, I could see running water, perhaps ocean water, in which blocks of ice were floating. I eventually noticed a light in the distance that increased in size. Then, other artificial lights began appearing. At this point, I was able to make out houses and lampposts.

With the helper at my side, we were soon entering a low-lying house resembling an apparatus-filled laboratory. Pictures could be seen hanging on a wall. There were two blond gentlemen, one of which was smoking continuously. They spoke very little, and what they did say was in English. It gave the impression of being a hothouse. I did not see any extraphysical consciousnesses, so I asked my traveling companion:

"Are there any projected consciousnesses here?"

"Yes, there are indeed. But there are very few intraphysical or extraphysical consciousnesses in this region."

Maps and graphs were scattered everywhere. One of the pictures showed an ice-breaker ship, with a navy officer standing at attention on its deck. All of the buildings in this polar region appeared to have been painted white for some inauguration. Everything seemed to be extremely clean.

On the way back, we met an extraphysical consciousness that performed assistance in the locale. I found it curious that he wore heavy clothes and thick huge boots, as if he were human and worked there in the frozen environment. I remained clad in my light pajamas. Incredible as it seemed, I was not affected in the least by the cold. There was no wind. It seemed like the air was still in an eternal, respectful silence.

Through mental dialogue, I learned that the extraphysical consciousness who assisted those men had physically died at that place long ago. He knew everything about that type of life, as he had lived it.

We saw an area where the inhabitants were exercising. Farther off, I could see a group of seals and some sea lions.

Since I was visiting this area in a projected state, I did not feel the bite of the cold. I realized that I did not find solitary frozen wastelands at all attractive. Life under such conditions can only be compared to an imposed exile. It must be an evolutionary necessity for the majority of those rare inhabitants who choose this lifestyle.

What was important in this case, was to recognize that multidimensional assistance exists everywhere, regardless of the adverse conditions of the environment.

We soon flew away from the area. In a short while, I returned to the air conditioned physical base.

After returning

I awoke in the soma and looked at the clock which read 2:47 a.m. In that same instant, the extraphysical events began to come to me in fragments, together with a shower of energy. I got up and, reaching for the thermometer hanging on the wall, saw that it read 79° F. Hurrah for the heat and the coming summer of Rio de Janeiro!

Observations

Following are some psychological processes that assist the projective beginner:

1. Maintain a burning desire to project yourself.

2. Permanently discard any fear of leaving the body.

3. Think intensely on the subject of projection.

4. Maintain awareness of the existence of your true self and the biological body.

5. Know everything possible about the psychosoma.

6. Visualize the "physical" route that the consciousness will follow once projected in the psychosoma outside the dense body.

7. Develop the habit of thinking about projection in the period immediately before sleeping.

8. Read about projection before sleeping.

9. Desire to dream about projection.

10. Saturate the mind with the idea of projection.

---

5 3 .   S P A C E   F L I G H T

Prior to projection

Friday, December 14, 1979. Third sleep at 11:04 p.m. Ambient temperature: 79° F. Humidity: 50%. I laid down on the left side, with no covers on top of the soma. Indirect air conditioning entered the room from the office.

Extraphysical period

My recollection of the projection starts from when I found myself alone and infinitely free in mid-air. I experienced a high degree of reasoning power and self-analytical capacity. I did not perceive any inconsistencies, incoherences or anachronisms in the circumstances!

I knew beyond the shadow of a doubt that I was projected. How did I get there? What had happened? I had no answers.

I looked up and saw the moon. It was bigger and clearer than usual. I felt the desire to fly towards it. I started to fly through space in the direction of the moon at an incredible rate.

I sensed the Earth becoming smaller behind me. I saw a few stars. Looking back, I felt so alone, isolated in the immensity of space, that I decided to return immediately, abandoning the target idea of reaching the moon. I was sure that, if I had wanted to, I would have soon been there.

Returning at great speed, I broke through a few clouds, similar to a plane descending, looking for a field to land in.

I was soon flying above several buildings. One of them, a lower one, had walls that were strengthened like a fortress. Descending further, I saw that it was the highest tower of a castle. It was deserted there on top. The night was profoundly tranquil. I could see a few lights from the city. I was not in Brazil.

From there, I passed over the roofs of several buildings and finally descended to street level. The spot was very pleasant. It resembled a clean, well constructed nativity scene. There was a calmness in the street, partly due to the late hour of the night. Few cars passed by on the roads. Only a few houses were lighted. Close to a triangular plaza were six parked taxis. They were not Brazilian vehicles. They seemed to be older and different. Near the cars, there was an open business with a lighted sign, which I did not read.

As I glided through the street, two female extraphysical consciousnesses noticed my psychosoma. I could not tell what language was spoken in that place, but I understood their thoughts. Upon examination, I confirmed that the psychosoma was present in its entirety, wearing a blue pajama top with three pockets. I found nothing special about my appearance. Maybe it was the v-neck or some visibility of the silver cord.

What happened next I do not recall. I know that I received a suggestion from somewhere to return to the soma. My mental control had been weakened. I suppose that I flew back to the apartment quickly. However, I have no recollection of it.

After returning

I next recall waking up. I was lying on the left side and the soma felt freezing cold. The nose was completely stuffed up in a condition of semi-suffocation. I changed positions, went to the bathroom and returned to bed. Looking at the clock, I noticed it was eleven minutes past midnight. The thermometer read 79°F. I then went through my projective routine. I laid down on the right side to sleep once more, covering myself with a white blanket.

Upon laying my head on the pillow, the extraphysical events arrived in fragments. The coldness of the soma had no doubt precipitated the return, affecting the awakening process and the recall of extraphysical events. This rarely happens to me.

Observation

Could it be that the long-distance projection in outer space contributed to the cooling down of the soma of flesh and bones? I do not think so. The maximum temperature reached this Friday was 103°F, the highest of this spring. This was a typical case of a delayed recall, which is an exception in common mnemonic processes.

---

54. SITTING IN MID-AIR

Prior to projection

Sunday, December 16, 1979. Energy emission exercises began at 7:07 p.m. A helper transmitted energy to the solar plexus area of the soma. It is worth noting that intestinal constipation with its consequent organic intoxication represents a serious obstacle to the process of projection. It hinders the circulation of energies below the diaphragm, especially in the splenic-chakra and umbilical-chakra. It also hinders the departure of the psychosoma from the solar plexus area. Furthermore, above the diaphragm, it reduces mental concentration as a result of increased salivation. It also causes the soma to become excessively restless, making it difficult to achieve a numbness of the physical body.

In the hypnagogic state, immediately before sleep, intestinal constipation predisposes the occurrence of physical repercussions. These are caused by the sudden return of an extraphysical arm or leg, when the psychosoma achieves only a partial non-alignment of the bodies, as a result of being held back by the solar plexus. In these cases it is always recommendable that energy emissions be applied to one's own abdominal area. These are executed by the projector or sponsored by a helper. The energy emissions neutralize the toxic effects, facilitating the natural progression of the projective process.

After performing energy exercises for some time, I got up to write and finally went back to bed at 11:22 p.m. The temperature was 79° F with indirect air conditioning. It was raining hard outside. The raindrops made a fair amount of noise as they hit the casing of the air conditioning. The wind whistled through the windows of the apartment high up in the building. The humidity was 54%. I laid down in the dorsal position, rigid, motionless and uncovered.

I remained inside the immobilized soma in a state of projective catalepsy for quite a while. Eventually, I started to feel the welling up of the powerful forces of the vibrational state. I felt like a generator, resonating as it produced power.

Extraphysical period

Deliberately disconnecting myself from the soma, I achieved a classical vertical takeoff. Within seconds I was in the psychosoma, which was directly above the soma.

The psychosoma became stabilized beneath the ceiling. I sat in mid-air, observing the situation and experiencing the powerful sensations of the vibrational cord that links the psychosoma to the soma.

My senses were sharper than usual and I started to think. It is not easy for one to deactivate their own soma, or in other words, to rupture the silver cord. It is very well established and stable. Still sitting in mid-air, I wanted to shift off to one side and then to another, but it was impossible. I was imprisoned by the body. There came to mind the sensation experienced by certain extra-physical consciousnesses who have suffered a recent deactivation of the soma. They have an identical experience of being conscious, wanting to leave, but not being able to do so. There are invisible links that hold and inhibit the freeing of the psychosoma.

I continued to philosophize, sitting in mid-air above the soma. It is fascinating to see how the projector knows with abso-lute certainty when he or she is projected! These natural sensations help to perfectly distinguish projections from dreams. I am simul-taneously the observer and a participant in the experience, wholly aware of events as they transpire.

I continued to reflect while projected. The projection of the psychosoma is an animic phenomenon. However, in a case such as this, while apparently provoking a lucid projection, I am certain of the presence of invisible assistance the whole time. Are psychic capacities involved in this process?

At that point I finally decided:

"I must get free. I will exit by leaping."

I gathered all my strength and, with all my will, leaped to the right into the hallway of the apartment. At that moment, a pleasant, pale, bluish light appeared that filled the whole room. The rooms had become huge, as if the walls had been pushed far-ther out.

I did not see any extraphysical consciousnesses, but was aware of being assisted by an intangible escort. I noticed that the space in the hallway was not the same as I recalled it to have been some two months before (chapter 32).

After reaching my son's bedroom, I immediately returned to the soma. I wanted to practice maintaining lucidity throughout the projective cycle, which is the most difficult feat to accomplish during projective experiences.

After returning

Laying down into the soma, the psychosoma was absorbed by it. Little by little, I began to experience the sensations of the soma. I opened the eyelids and ended the numbness. I was able to follow the entire process without losing awareness at any time.

I looked at the clock. It was 24 minutes past midnight; it was already Monday. The rain continued to fall noisily outside.

55. *KALEIDOSCOPES OF DESIRES*

Prior to projection

Monday, December 17, 1979. Temperature: 79°F. Humidity: 62%. After receiving some instructions from Transmentor through psychophonic monologue, I laid down in the dorsal position at 7:12 p.m.

The soma began to get numb, and an invisible hand began pressing down on the forehead. Next, there was a buildup of pressure at the base of the skull and I remember nothing else of the waking state.

Extraphysical period

I first recalled entering an extraphysical organization. There was a vast hall with various split levels and a congregation of more than 500 extraphysical children between the ages of 2 and 13. The extraphysical consciousnesses had the appearance of real children with infantile mentalities. Many resembled angels. Others were not so attractive for various reasons, including the effects resulting from diseases and deformities.

The whole extraphysical complex was similar to a covered playground with a very high ceiling. Here, the energy of the ambiance was doubtless better than the average energetic pattern of its mini-inhabitants.

The little ones were generally well behaved. They all paid attention to the show that was going on above their heads. It was like a fireworks show but, instead of having exploding stars, balls of light and multi-colored streamers, there were fantastic kaleidoscopes or galaxies materializing dreams and wishes, breathing life into toys, machines and three-dimensional fantasies.

I understood that the creations were incredibly vivid and real morphothosenes, the products of powerful consciousnesses. There were magic wands opening treasure chests, Santa Claus sacks, cornucopias of riches, surprise boxes, magic lamps, videos of endless stories and everlasting springs of wonders, satisfying the most exotic whims. The images were incredibly rich, beautiful and extravagant.

I was witnessing the result of the capacity of conscious-nesses to produce elaborate objects through the use of extraphysical "substances." Behind it all, there was more than likely a battalion of inventive and experienced Carnots (chapter 2), working intensely. I did not perceive any apparatus. It all seemed to appear out of nothing.

I thought about how the vast, complex extraphysical dimension presents infinite possibilities for exploration, and is still awaiting its "Colombuses," explorers, pioneers and researchers to reveal it entirely.

The spectacle I was witnessing served as a kind of fortifying injection to the imagination of the children. It had the effect of enhancing their intelligence and promoting a greater maturity of the consciousness.

The toys rained down on the little ones with mirth, melodies, dances, mysteries, tenderness and love in their forms and movements, and would disappear just before touching the children's heads. If a child was interested, the object of his or her desire would materialize in his or her hands. Everything seemed to be appearing out of thin air.

The institution contained amusement parks, a circus with ponies, fountains of toys, orchards of Christmas trees, imagination projectors, a thousand-and-one inventions and everything that the consciousness has ever conceived and created. All of it pulsing with life, light, animation, dimension and beauty, originating and spiraling in an incessant act of creation. The extraphysical children were fascinated. Therein lay the secret of their apparent tranquillity. The show had a soothing effect through its magnitude and grandeur, by exciting the children's imagination. Soon, each child held their desired objects as if they had received prizes and trophies.

Curiously, the most advanced story was narrated in mid-air. I witnessed vehicles and structures of all types rain down from incredibly beautiful multicolored clouds in a seemingly endless flow of overwhelmingly harmonious, inspiring narratives that followed one another in multiple, coexisting, interpenetrating scenarios.

I find it difficult to describe what I saw that night. After re-reading what I have written about the experience, I find the description quite pale in comparison to the reality of the magnificent, multifaceted spectacle that I witnessed. What more can I do with words?

I wish to register a few important details. Many dark-skinned children were completely translucent as a result of so much light. One of the children in better condition assisted other smaller, unbalanced children. I noticed that the majority of extraphysical consciousnesses at that stage of infantile human appearance did not fly. Outside of that sort of covered stadium, were incredibly beautiful, sprawling gardens.

Based on my deductions, the mental recuperation of the extraphysical consciousnesses at that locale appears to be quick. However, I do not think they will all directly resume extraphysical adulthood. Many will embark on another intraphysical life with a lot of extraphysical growing up still to do. The extraphysical ambiance was profoundly pleasant. I perceived more sound there in the mental transmissions than I normally do when outside the body. This is perhaps the extraphysical locale where I have heard the greatest intensity of sound.

I recall flying away from there extremely happy, but do not remember arriving at the apartment.

After returning

I woke up in the numb soma. The joints seemed to be dehydrated. It was 8:43 p.m.

56. PROOF OF THE MENTALSOMA

Prior to projection

Wednesday, December 19, 1979. I laid in the dorsal position at 3:53 a.m., after having written for some time in the office. Temperature: 77°F. Humidity: 72%. Phase of the moon: new at 5:24 a.m.

Extraphysical period

Now completely alert and monitoring all psychic perceptions, I experienced the vibrational state and finally decided to leave the soma in a vertical takeoff.

After some time, I left the soma through the physical head. The psychosoma remained inside the soma. I knew it and could feel it. Light, coming from no particular source, bathed the environment. At this point, my visual capacities became greatly enhanced.

Trying to maintain my role as an observer, I examined the wall past the end of the bed, which appeared to be taller and more distant. Due to the light, I was not able to see the three posters hanging on the wall. They were probably hidden in whole or in part by the bright light. The extraphysical illumination was more intense and vibrant than usual. I made a mental note:

"I am aware of being able to see everything above and behind me, even though I am not totally projected. I am a lone consciousness, separate from everything, bodiless and alive."

At this point, I became aware of the situation and affirmed:

"Here is proof of the existence and capacity of the mentalsoma. It is capable of moving on its own! I am really an extraphysical consciousness without a body. I am completely in the mentalsoma with the consciousness mobile inside the bedroom!"

This had been a target idea of mine for a long time: to experience the isolated presence of the liberated consciousness, acting with lucidity without the psychosoma. I continued to look at the wall, seeing the soma's head, trunk, arms and legs stretched out, rigid, shining intensely on the left side of the king-size bed, when I witnessed the exit of the right arm of the psychosoma. It produced an intense phosphorescent-like glare. It shook and oscillated upwards. Then, the left arm of the psychosoma raised itself out in the same fashion. Both extraphysical arms continued to oscillate. Even the fingers vibrated, shimmering like candle flames. The extraphysical arms were bare, without pajama sleeves, unlike the soma, which was clothed. At this point, had the head of the psychosoma already reached me? I could not tell with any degree of certainty. I think the psychosoma was leaving the soma, finding its way towards the mentalsoma which, in turn, accepted it. What type of connection promotes such a process?

I returned to the soma and immediately resumed the waking state. To a great extent this occurred against my will. Nevertheless, I maintained lucidity throughout.

It all happened in the period of a few brief moments. I did not observe the silver cord, nor did I notice the formation of any energetic "smoke" or "fog" around the soma, as sometimes occurs. I recalled everything that had transpired in this ephemeral projection. The legs and trunk of the psychosoma, including the solar plexus, had not left the soma. The parts of the psychosoma that had separated never quite stabilized outside the soma.

In my case, it is very rare that the extraphysical head, together with the mentalsoma, exit the soma before the limbs and trunk of the psychosoma. I usually feel the separation of the psychosoma in the reverse order, with the extraphysical eyelids remaining closed inside the soma, allowing me to see nothing. This illustrates that takeoff and return can occur in various manners, with two basic types of projection – of the isolated mentalsoma and of the psychosoma as well, in the same occasion. What occurs on any one occasion, depends upon the factors influencing the process at the time. What factors were involved this night? One factor must have been the low density of the psychosoma.

The exit of the extraphysical head from the soma while in alignment with the mentalsoma in a partial non-alignment of the bodies had allowed me to perceive the extraphysical illumination. I did not detect the presence of any helpers at the time.

After returning

I was soon moving the soma. I looked at the clock. It was 4:01 am. The projection had lasted 8 minutes.

Observations

The controlling of one's own thoughts while projected is of utmost importance. The projector should always maintain awareness of his projected condition in order to derive full benefit from the extraphysical experience. For example: becoming excessively absorbed in a fact or subject while projected in the psychosoma, one can become emotional and end up losing control of the experience. This can reduce our lucidity and can even provoke a premature return to the soma. It can also compromise the recall of extraphysical events.

There were two distinct types of return in this projection. First, the attraction of the psychosoma to the projected mentalsoma. Second, the routine return of the psychosoma to the soma. This was a mixed projection in that both the mentalsoma and parts of the psychosoma were projected from the soma.

57. FRATERNAL LESSON

Prior to projection

Wednesday, December 19, 1979. Temperature: 77°F. Humidity: 68%. I laid down in the dorsal position at 10:11 p.m.

Extraphysical period

I found myself lucid outside the soma, being taken a long distance by a friend to another country on another continent. Here, an extraphysical consciousness met me and recommended that I confidently follow close behind her wherever she went, and not leave her company.

The extraphysical female appeared to be constantly focused and unshakably serene. She wore the simple outfit of a monk. I felt a most pleasant flow of energy while in her presence. An indescribable sensation of freedom and a sense of fraternity overcame me. I experienced an incredibly well contained sense of exaltation. In spite of being on the planetary crust, the psychosoma was uncommonly light. I immediately felt that I was in the presence of a very evolved consciousness. Everything about her inspired harmony and well-being. I would soon discover, however, that she was suffering deep inside through her compassion for human pain. As I tried to get closer to this extraphysical consciousness, I began to experience the pain of the world deep within me.

We arrived at an area of extreme poverty, having houses and small yards with shrunken trees. The very primitive and poor nature of this environment was quite evident in the bright daylight.

The extraphysical consciousness rarely stood up. She would remain sitting in a typical cross-legged yoga position, even while flying, perhaps trying to administrate her energies through meditation. Her movements were limited almost entirely to calmly moving her arms.

I tried to do the same, as far as I was able, wherever we went.

We went to dozens of huts and makeshift shelters in difficult to reach rural areas where the extraphysical benefactor visited the sick. The areas visited included: an open field where a crowd was gathered; a type of orphanage for sick children; an institution of apparently catholic sisters; an overcrowded prison of dirty, unshaven men dressed in rags and living in great promiscuity.

Wherever she went, the all-understanding, all-knowing messenger spread inspiration and energies of healing, peace and fraternity. While beside her, I felt filled with compassion, jubilation, tenderness, understanding, humanity, abnegation and all elevated and constructive ideas and sentiments. Wherever we went, the extraphysical consciousnesses present would back away from the approaching helper in reverent silence. This reaction was exhibited by rebellious intruders and mentally disturbed beings alike.

I did not witness any energetic confrontations or any of the usual cleansing and extraphysical assistance. It seemed like the mere arrival of this emissary of good will would sweep away misfortune and cleanse the consciousnesses and their environment. The power of pure love is fantastic!

I do not know how to express the profound nature of what I experienced during the excursion with this helper. It was a true trajectory of light and peace.

I am intrigued by the fact that she asked no questions – she simply assisted. She arrived knowing everything about everyone, and improved individuals and their environment as if by magic.

Once more, extraphysical facts confirm that emotionality constitutes an unbalance and is counterproductive, whereas serenity is synonymous with balance and evolution. It is strange how tranquil pure love is.

As some malevolent humans came into sight next to a structure, I could see a few objects resembling weapons. The extraphysical consciousness simply stretched out her arms and, within seconds, the entire mass began to burn slowly, until everything had disappeared and the fire extinguished itself. All that was left were dark marks from the flames. How can we explain this event within the framework of known laws? It constitutes the greatest evidence that dense matter and extraphysical objects are derived from the same source. We humans lack the know-how, as well as the energy to manifest wonders without violating universal principles.

Projection allows one to encounter a wide range of completely unpredictable supernormal experiences. What extraordinary energy does a superior consciousness possess? What personal effort was necessary in order for this stellar vortex of extraphysical cleansing and assistance to arrive at her level of development?

An infant, only days old, at the orphanage received special assistance from the extraphysical consciousness. The baby girl received a transmission of energy so powerful that she appeared to grow as I watched. Upon walking into the room, a nurse noticed the difference in the physical condition of the newborn child and happily carried her into the yard.

A seven-year-old child at the same institution detected the presence of the helper. She became radiant with joy and kept staring at her until the extraphysical consciousness placed a hand on her head out of compassion. The child smiled happily and left the room, singing and dancing.

During the entire extraphysical experience I did not perceive the extraphysical consciousness to engage in transmental dialogue. She did not waste a single moment, but continued to assist in many different ways, acting as a source of pure affection for all types of creatures in all conditions from all origins. This was perhaps the biggest lesson in pure fraternity that I have received in this life. The extraphysical consciousness was well aware of it as I bid farewell in silence with my thoughts of gratitude.

After returning

I awoke in the soma and cried deeply felt tears for a few minutes, when I remembered to look at the clock. Human life had to go on. It was 11:43 p.m. I got up to register the extraphysical events, which came to me with undisturbed clarity.

---

58.   COMBAT IN THE RAVINE

Prior to projection

Wednesday, December 26, 1979. I laid down on the left side. Second sleep at 12:09 a.m. Temperature: 77°F. Humidity: 72%.

Extraphysical period

I became lucid next to an extraphysical consciousness with the appearance of a tall woman. Judging by her extraphysical features, she was about six feet tall and a yard wide! She nevertheless seemed very pleasant and was dressed in white. I felt that this helper had provoked my extraphysical awakening through energy transmissions. She sent me an extremely high-speed mental communication that we were going to an area of ravines. Within moments we were landing next to an enormous gorge in a ravine.

The extraphysical consciousness remained in front of me. I could observe her from behind. When I focused on her hair, she reminded me of someone I had met in my childhood. The extraphysical consciousness was quite evolved and energetically vigorous.

Pointing to the deep ravine, she asked me to examine the environment, bid me farewell, and disappeared suddenly.

I was in a place that appeared to be somewhere in the intraphysical dimension. There was a localized storm a short distance before me in the ravine. Strange colored blotches and nauseating smells bubbled up from the water resulting from the storm. I focused my extraphysical vision and was able to distinguish what was going on.

As incredible as it might seem, two extraphysical consciousnesses were fighting each other in a continuous battle. There were so many continuously changing deformations in their figures that they gave the impression of: shapeless amoebas devouring each other; inextinguishable continuously inter-exploding fire bombs; living flames in a raging fire; dragons gridlocked in a bloody fight, making unpleasant guttural sounds. The combatants changed their stances and positions with lightning speed. The exotic, unstable life forms changed from one unpleasant color to another.

The beasts' melancholic show inspired simultaneous repulsion and compassion in me. They were being watched by a group of whimsical, agitated consciousnesses. Questions arose in my mind. What should I do? How long would it last?

At that moment, I heard a resonating voice:

"A battle such as this is the sad epilogue in the conflict between these two consciousnesses. It will continue until the two opponents become exhausted, end up losing their humanoid forms and become enclosed in their own private world."

I continued to watch the scene, musing that I had never thought, seen or read of anything like it. The voice then transmitted some thoughts:

"In the initial stages of the battle, when the opponents still have sufficient energy and their efforts are more spectacular, spectators frequently appear who become agitated by the morbid event, as they hunger for strong emotions. This is what is happening here. The opponents, moved by the fire of hatred and manipulated by the power of unbalanced minds, will continue to gradually change until their forms regress. This constitutes a temporary suicide for these two who are poisoned through a malfunctioning of their higher mental faculties. Have thoughts and sentiments of peace for all these demented beings and go on your way."

I emitted thoughts and energies of peace and fraternity for all those gathered there, and tried to understand the bizarre event. It was the biggest energetic confrontation that I have ever witnessed outside of the body. About all I could do was to pity those concerned.

I did not have any critical emotional reaction from watching the sad combat. This led me to observe:

"What a difference, compared to other occasions. If we ourselves change so much from projection to projection, what differences can we expect to find from projector to projector?"

Everyone has their own energetic capacity. Once outside the soma, one will perceive extraphysical events in his own way, such that two projectors will never have identical experiences or results. The extraphysical dimension is a mental world. The mental universe of each one of us is unique and different from that of others.

Now at the side of the ravine, I decided to follow the voice's suggestion. I flew up and away from the field, which I was able to see, even from a distance. Now far from the ravine, I flew between the clouds through waves of energy, which acted like turbulence and impeded my flight. Nevertheless, I experienced an immense sense of well-being due to the freedom from the soma. Nothing can be compared to flying in an open space every once in a while: thinking and acting away from the limitations of a dense body. I was in a perfect state of mind: happy, tranquil, and yet without euphoria.

It took a lot longer to return than it did to go. Within minutes, I was back at the apartment, passing through the bedroom window. The psychosoma re-entered the soma smoothly.

My lucidity was not affected by the waking process. I was not at all sleepy, but was more aware after the projection than I had been before.

After returning

The clock showed 12:42 am. It started to rain outside. Could the rain clouds have caused the waves of turbulence?

59.   A PERTINENT QUESTION

Prior to projection

Thursday, December 27, 1979. I laid down on the right side
for my second sleep. It was 12:03 a.m. The rain fell noisily against
the window. Temperature: 77°F. Humidity: 72%.

Extraphysical period

I found myself in the lobby of an unfamiliar hotel, admiring
the flowers of an indoor garden. I did not see any helpers. Were
they assisting someone in the hotel? My vision was incredibly
clear. I wanted to explore the outside of the hotel. I had apparently
not prepared any theme of study. Hurling myself against a tall
glass panel, I quickly passed through it into mid-air. I began to fly
and passed through a group of singing birds. I thought to myself:

"It is not raining here. In fact it is a beautiful day. It must be
five or six o'clock in the morning."

I concluded that I was not in Brazil, based on the obvious
difference in the weather. No longer a prisoner of the soma, I felt
omniscient as I went through walls and flew through the air using
and appreciating the amplified powers of the projected consciousness. I affirmed with conviction:

"I need to control my thoughts, because I do not want to return yet."

I made this suggestion to myself, as it is sometimes difficult
to control one's thoughts completely during a projection.

I continued to fly through the blue sky when I saw a kind of
farm below me. In awe, I exclaimed:

"How beautiful it all is!"

The colors, the plants, the irrigation canals, the fences, the
roads, everything about the scenery seemed like a postcard chosen
from thousands of others.

I flew over the farm, choosing to operate with the sincere
interest of the investigator as opposed to the spirit of the adven-
turer. I decided to fly down lower in order to examine the constructions among the trees. I saw a huge cow with natural roundish

spots. It struck me as odd that the cow seemed to emit light from its entire soma through the skin as it ate inside the well kept barn.

I saw a tall, beautiful, brownish horse nearby. As I came close, it raised its head and flared its nostrils. I got closer and sent thoughts to the horse, as if whispering kind words. I passed the right extraphysical hand over its head and could feel the heat of its body. The beautiful animal, now satisfied, quieted down. I was now just like any other man of flesh and bones to it. I circled the whole area and decided to go back to my apartment.

After returning

Upon finding myself back in the soma, I opened the eyelids and consulted the clock. It was 12:45 a.m. and still raining, just as it had been when I had left. I got up to register the events with the satisfaction of having performed a good quick voyage abroad.

The factors that most influence the quality of a projection are one's thoughts immediately before takeoff, the condition of the soma, and one's emotions while in the extraphysical dimension.

It was 2:26 a.m. when I went back to bed. I laid down in the dorsal position and felt the onset of another projection. I felt as though something like an iron helmet covered the ears and the entire skull.

Extraphysical period

I felt that I was outside the soma, but could not see properly. I thought intensely about seeing, and a soft light appeared everywhere. I was now more lucid than I had been in the preceding waking state. I found myself inside an enormous hall with many people.

A tall, tanned, young male extraphysical consciousness was standing next to the exit door of the hall. He got my attention and I approached him. Upon recognizing him, I greeted him and mentally asked:

"Do you remember me?"

"Yes. From the Center. Have you been dead a long time?"

I laughed and immediately answered this most uncommon question:

"Me, no! I am alive. I am a person. I live in Rio de Janeiro and am projected right now."

The young extraphysical consciousness, an old acquaintance from Uberaba, opened his eyes wide as if shining light through them. I added:

"Isn't it incredible? I will return to my soma and remember all this."

The young man raised his right hand to his mouth in a very human manner, as if in disbelief. I cheerily transmitted a further mental explanation:

"Here I am more or less like you. Watch this: I will walk through that man over there."

I went towards a man who had just finished lighting a cigarette while talking to someone in the well-lighted street. I passed through him within seconds. I returned to the young man and further demonstrated the penetrability of the bodies:

"Here is how you trip him!"

I passed the right leg of the psychosoma through the legs of the same man twice in a row, as if kicking him in the shins, in a simple simulation of a physical action. The man did not show any awareness of my presence.

The young male consciousness, whose name I did not recall, started to laugh as I bid him farewell with a final embrace. I also laughed, feeling as if I were an extraphysical practical joker. I did not recognize this area which was outside of Rio de Janeiro. I soon returned to the physical base.

After returning

I opened the eyelids reluctantly. If I had wished, I could have left the soma again, but I preferred to write down the still vivid extraphysical events in their every detail before I could forget them, as I did not want to lose them. The clock showed 3:43 a.m. It was raining lightly outside. I did not see the helper who had assisted me. I wanted to thank him for the successful high quality experiments and the incredible consistency of the observations.

Observations

The simple fact that a lucid extraphysical consciousness mistook me for another extraphysical consciousness lent more credibility to the projective experiences than any other detail. Had this mistaken conclusion occurred due to the psychosoma being in a condition of lower density?

Following is a brief analysis of the technical contents of this book. Some of this data is original, and has never been presented in the field of projective research. I did not find any indication that the day of the week interfered with the success of the projections. I experienced projections on all days of the week. In some periods I had more projections during certain days of the week, but this did not continue over a long period of time. However, over the time period considered for this book, there were more projections on Wednesdays and fewer on Mondays.

The projections related here were taken from a series that reached a frequency of one per day over a period of 163 days, a period of slightly less than six months. They rarely occurred on alternating (every other) days. Sundays and holidays were not taken into account as part of the overall period. From the frequency of the projections, it is possible to appreciate the intensity of the extraphysical tasks.

A factor which has an obvious influence on the time at which the projections will take place is the work schedule of the projector. Consecutive projections took place on several average days of the week. There were some days of the week on which I did not project. This varied from month to month, specifically: Mondays, Fridays and Saturdays in August; Mondays and Saturdays in September; Mondays, Tuesdays and Fridays in October; Sundays and Tuesdays in November. This data presents nothing particularly significant. The following projections took place either in the early morning or at night, at the beginning and end of a 24 hour period: July 25 (chapter 6 and 7), December 19 (chapters 56 and 57).

In certain periods, my schedule allowed a high frequency of projections. For example: the 9 projections described in chapters 2-10 took place over 12 consecutive days in July; the 10 projections related in chapters 48-57 occurred over 13 consecutive days in December. The great majority of projections took place during the "period of human anguish", between 6:00 and 10:00 p.m. This is to be expected, given the assistential nature of the services rendered by the helpers.

The phase of the moon did not seem to have any particularly observable effect. This indicates that so-called planetary influences do not affect projections.

The soma does not generally move while the psychosoma is projected. I always found the soma in the same position that I had left it in. The length of time away from the soma averaged one hour.

With respect to the position of the projector's soma, there was a definite predominance of the dorsal position, the best position of all. I found that pointing the head in the direction of geographical north had no effect.

The ambient temperature generally ranged between 68° and 77°F.

The sex life of the projector was maintained in perfect harmony with the projections and the activities of the helpers.

Several types of projections took place during the period of observation. prolonged projections: chapters 6, 7, 24, 36, 38 and 51; brief projections: chapters 30, 32, 35, 54 and 56; consecutive projections: chapters 3, 25, 27, 30, 32, 39, 41, 50 and 59; projections preparing the projector for other projections: chapters 38, 39 and 41; partial projections: chapters 23, 32, 50 and 56; self-projections or those voluntarily induced by the projector: chapters 23, 30, 31, 45 and 50; projections arising from the augmented vision of the psychosoma: chapters 8 and 31; projections within a 13-foot radius of the soma and therefore under the intense influence of the silver cord: chapters 20, 32 and 35; recurrent projection to a specific location: chapter 31; projections guided by extra-physical consciousnesses: chapters 32, 41 and 47; cleansing projections: chapters 15, 27 and 44; daytime projection: chapter 42; nighttime projections: the majority of the experiences described.

Three projections of the mentalsoma were executed (chapters 19, 56 and 60). The existence of dimensions of various natures can generally be observed. These vary according to the energetic density of the environment and the conditions of the psychosoma of the inhabitants. There are extraphysical locales that interpenetrate the earth's crust (chapter 20); colonies where it was difficult to fly (chapters 12 and 51); a terrestrial area allowing unrestricted flight (chapters 17, 21 and others); dimensions without form or time (chapter 60).

Some projections showed that the condition of the psychosoma varies according to one's level of mental equilibrium and will-power (chapters 1, 3, 20, 22, 29, 30, 51, 60 and others). In some cases, mind-to-mind communication occurred freely (chapters 3, 9, 18 and others); and in other cases with reception problems (chapter 24).

Thus, we can see that there are consciousnesses who are worse off as extraphysical consciousnesses than they would be if they were in the intraphysical state. This illustrates the value of intraphysical life. Also, there are extraphysical ambiances that our finite mind is not able to comprehend while imprisoned in the physical brain.

These observations lead to a general conclusion. The consciousness expresses itself through its thosenes. Thought gives rise to decisions, action and the transport of the consciousness. The control of one's own thoughts constitutes self-control. Therefore, there are extraphysical consciousnesses and projected persons who are more-or-less luminous, that breathe or do not breathe, who do or do not use articulated speech, who suffer the influence of time, gravitation, form and space, habits and instincts, and conditioned reflexes. All this depends on the degree of one's inner lucidity which is inversely proportional to the amount of one's dense energy, consequently leaving one with a higher or lower degree of density. In this way, we determine our own evolutionary stature, either as animals living on this planetary crust (man is, after all, an animal) or as cosmic beings on the path towards the infinite.

60. FREE CONSCIOUSNESS

Prior to projection

Thursday, January 25, 1979[1]. Second sleep at 12:20 a.m. at the usual physical base in the bedroom of the apartment in Ipanema, Rio de Janeiro. I had initially gone to bed at 11:15 p.m., like any other night. I felt some physical fatigue as I laid down on the left side. No energy emission exercises took place. I also do not have any recollection of the takeoff.

Extraphysical period

I became lucid in an evolved extraphysical region, the splendor and beauty of which transcended the locales typically found on the Earth's crust. I saw only lights and vivid colors of indefinite shapes. The site appeared to be completely uninhabited. There were no dwellings in sight. My experience was that of simply existing as a consciousness. I did not feel the form of the psychosoma. It was invisible even to me.

Lighter than usual outside the dense body, I had an attitude of confidence and moral superiority, which made unequivocally sublime energies arise within me, in an indefinable, tranquil contentment.

There were no human forms or faces, only centers of energy radiation constituting familiar consciousnesses, some of which were noteworthy by their deeds, such as the psychics Fernando de Lacerda, Aura Celeste and Eusápia Paladino. All of them had been converted into pure light. They had no names, nor were they identifiable by their forms, but I knew them and was united with them through common experiences. I was suddenly sure of being a participant in a formless gathering, composed of bodiless points of mental focus, of masses of energy that was taking place in a *nirvanic* atmosphere that was of an unimaginable level of mental elevation, unapproachable with Earthly descriptions, and indefinable in known terms.

---

[1]This projection has been taken out of this diary's otherwise chronological order.

Were my imperfect perceptions influenced by the perfect environment? How can I say the unspeakable, describe the indescribable, beyond prose, poetry, and conventional word play? How can I find the language of origins, the common denominator, the universal level, in order to situate myself in that formless assembly, to understand this non-anthropomorphic group and penetrate their unyielding mysteries?

In that dimension, only the mentalsomas of those consciousnesses vibrated. A single fact stood out. That was my exact knowledge of who each one was in that place that does not exist in time, but will exist in *eternity*. There, in that nonexistent place, nothing existed, but everything was existing. I experienced "touchable" ideas, unshakable certainties, indescribable serenity and undreamed of well-being.

It was clear that a Higher Consciousness would manifest itself through everyone present. This indeed occurred, slowly and smoothly.

The thosenes of that intangible consciousness having unimaginable attributes, projected my consciousness to the apex of sentiment, with great impact. The experience affected and then replaced the very structure of my emotions.

Devoid of commotion or euphoria, that definitive structural peace told me that this reality constitutes the most impactful event of intraphysical life. It is worth everything, including any sacrifice necessary, to be able to experience "that" which comes from someone who has reached the highest level of evolution. How can I express it? How can I even give the reader an idea of it? How can I describe it? "Who" will I describe? Now, more than ever, I experience the utter inadequacy of words and expressions. A drop of water in the sun, a galactic explosion of peace, a cosmic avalanche without a fall, a universe without limits, an ocean current in a drop of sea water? Mere words. It is impossible to describe something that does not have a point of reference. One can not establish boundaries for the infinite.

One thing was certain: it was a free consciousness. A lucid vortex of vibrant energetic emanation; free from matter, form and space; free from the series of rebirths onto the Earth's crust; no longer possessing a psychosoma in the usual sense.

Are all free consciousnesses alike in their evolutionary multiple genius? They are at a stage of evolution that is inconceivable from our planetary point of reference, in conditions unappreciable by the human brain, with universal sentiments inaccessible to us with our perceptions, traditions and conditioning.

What name? Who? From where? The label is inconsequential. What form? Is there form? How to understand? Let the contemporary student of evolution be the one to choose a name. Ray of light, photon, nonexistent point, anti-energy, pre-God? Behold the simple and yet utterly complex.

A constant "nirvanic orgasm" cast those consciousnesses present into the peace of the nebulous whirl. Each consciousness appeared to have the potential to proliferate a large portion of the universe, being the center and the periphery, a part and the whole. A creator in action. Each personality present, both extraphysical and intraphysical consciousnesses, lived the indescribable momentum.

The eloquence of the dissertation that apparently did not take place, spoken in the silent voice of the inner self, appeared fleeting, and yet everlasting. The influx emanated from an invisible, nonphysical superhuman consciousness with a serene knowledge, and no emotionalism.

The message emphasized the benefits of putting to use the experience acquired by mature persons in order to assist younger persons to avoid wasting the multifaceted knowledge of those same elderly individuals, taking into account the rising increase and predominance of youthful humans in the current terrestrial period.

Due to an intellectual expansion, a tranquilizing, supra-physical, supra-rational erudite certainty arose. I did not hear anything, and there had been no common thought transmission.

I sensed and understood everything down to the last detail, at once. Someone had been there, who no one had seen, but who all had noticed. A message had been transmitted that no one had heard, but all had understood.

After returning

Upon returning to the soma, I cried sobs of innermost comprehension and shed the tears of indescribable euphoria of one who wants to make the world a happy place, inundating the Earth, if possible, with the melody of those sobs and the sweetness of those tears.

Observations

Even with my experience in automatic writing, channeling, clairvoyance, precognition, physical effects and many hundreds and various types of projections, I have experienced nothing in this life that compares to the wonders of the "sightless vision" and "emotion of structural peace" that was "seen" and "felt" in this fully conscious projection using the mentalsoma. My life is now divided into two parts: before and after this projection. It was an incomparable milestone, and a moment of great peace.

The clock showed 12:42 a.m. How can I determine the duration of that gathering? The passing of time had nothing to do with the experience. Time had ceased to exist. In 22 minutes of sleep, I had experienced a millennium of reality. A few moments had passed, that were worth centuries. A second had proven to be worth a millennium. This projection, having a curious distortion of the time-space continuum, had gone from a temporal and spatial level to the cosmic level – beyond all material restrictions and physical impediments.

It all happened with the naturality of a sunrise, family life, a running brook, tall green grass swaying in the wind, birds singing, a calm sea, clouds in a blue sky – but it was all so transcendent. This fact impregnated my mind with the certainty of basic truths making them innate to my very being.

My wish to remain there overrode all other desires and aspirations, but an irresistible command ordered me to return and continue my intraphysical life. A desire arose to leave the soma behind for that glorious, peaceful, swirling dimension, unknown yet known, indescribable. Reason, however, would never allow me to relax my enthusiasm for acting with dignity up until the deactivation of the soma. My major commitments compelled me to continue intraphysical life with the profound happiness of the certainty of seeing the near future, present-future or present-already-future, within the relative illusion of terrestrial time, knowing that the future, depending on my efforts, will be a conquest to be permanently enjoyed.

After the vision, I felt like a superman, but a superman without violence, without uncertainties, without any desire to compromise, only thinking, speaking and doing whatever is possible for the welfare of everything and everyone with an absolutely-certain-optimism, a sweet-contained-euphoria, and a conviction-indignation with myself. I lost any bitterness towards the past-present-future, people-animals-facts-things and circumstances. Now at peace with all, I sensed that I would encounter other contractual responsibilities. Given my current developmental level, at what point in the future – in which intraphysical life, during which intermissive course – will I have another identical vision? It will depend on personal effort. It will always be that way for everyone.

Before I experienced this vision, nature, astronomy, astronautics, so-called flying saucers, science fiction, physics, classical music and the imaginative fantasies of the great artists were, for me, the most impressive examples of the evolution of the consciousness. Now, with all due admiration and respect, they appear to be very crude and rudimentary. Compared to a future beyond time and form, they all disappear like a theater set as it tumbles to the ground.

More than ever, there is justification for the existence of philosophy and poetry as the only lines of thought for the intraphysical mind that are capable of freeing one from transitory human deficiency. This allows one to satisfy the burning desire of expanding oneself closer to timeless realities. Never did the importance of the Revelation on rational studies emanate so deeply from within me. The fourteen billion cells in the brain allow only an infinitesimal, filtered version of the reality of free consciousness, irrespective of how extensively one has developed one's mental capacities, imagination, critical judgment, or the millions of existent specialized cortical zones and cerebral connections, groupings, interactions and interdependencies.

Is it possible to have this experience or vision repeatedly as a normal extraphysical occurrence? Does man's biological mechanism possess resources capable of resisting the impacts of that "peace" or "well being"? Throughout the centuries of human history, psychics inconsistently used mysticism and rituals as personal crutches or emotional escapes from the realities that they experienced. Or perhaps they intuited how to better support their soma from that point on. But that resource is not the ideal. There was no trace of mysticism in this manifestation of free consciousness.

I now feel that I better understand the panoramic life review that terminally ill patients and recently deceased consciousnesses experience. They experience a projection beyond time and space within the integral memory bank of the consciousness, similar to an immense computer able to instantaneously access its autobiographical records using all of its resources. The free mind unites the past, the present and the future into a single reality. Projection of the consciousness triggers, when one is outside of the soma, the most extensively altered state of the consciousness, which sometimes affects the biogravitational field and even acts on the curvature of space, allowing thought to travel faster than the speed of light.

Extraphysical ecstasy, which has received so much commentary over the centuries, pales in comparison to the reality of the vision of free consciousness. There are expansions of emotion and repercussions of ideas far superior to ecstasy, illumination, temporary, formless super-consciousness, and profound *samadhi* or cosmic consciousness. The consciousness controls matter and its apparently immutable laws, beyond all space, time, sentiments, thoughts, expectations or comprehension of change.

As for myself, the soma, holo-chakra, silver cord, psychosoma and its transformations, expansions of the consciousness, as well as the mentalsoma, or the consciousness when acting alone, are facts, as I have already experienced them. Based on this, I think that the mentalsoma represents the permanent condition that free consciousness finds itself in.

This projection also demonstrated a curious fact. Intraphysical and extraphysical consciousnesses utilizing the mentalsoma can function as intermediaries in the extraphysical dimension.

Imitating the astronomer who is capable of predicting the existence of an unknown celestial body through gravitational laws and the orbital paths of planets and stars, we can also apply the same analogous principle to extraphysical studies. In biology we have the concept of homogeneity whose definition is "similarity of structure and origin in parts and organisms taxonomically different". We know for sure that between the soma of a mother and another soma belonging to a fetus, there exists an initial constant connection of the umbilical cord. Similarly, we do not ignore that between the intraphysical and extraphysical bodies there exists the silver cord, a second semi-physical, tangible constant connection which, in certain aspects, has volume and occupies space. Is it possible through homogeneity that there exists a third connection, a constant, ethereal or quintessential cord of another nature between the psychosoma and the mentalsoma? Where? How? Of what nature?

I offer this hypothesis and topic of research for future projectors and researches. If this supposition is correct, it clearly explains: that rebirth occurs upon the cutting of the umbilical cord; that deactivation of the soma occurs with the cutting of the silver cord; and that the appearance of free consciousness, in the act of discarding the psychosoma or emotional body, occurs with the "rupture" of the quintessential cord or "golden cord", leaving only the mentalsoma.

In the same manner, we can give the name of mentalsoma to the consciousness when acting alone in a temporary fashion, and the denomination of *causal body* to the consciousness when permanently acting alone, or the condition which we call free consciousness.

Thus, we can see that the "rebirths" of the consciousness are multiple and varied. But this constitutes only a secondary question of words or names in the interest of clarity.

A vision of this nature causes the vivacity of thought to give a better idea of the profoundness of the past and the infinity of the future, reaching, revolving and interacting in all directions. Incoherences, contradictions and paradoxes disappear. Extremely clear thoughts arise in all areas. The impossible becomes reality. One is able to identify, more than ever, the deficiencies of the instinctive cerebral cortex and its influences on rational acts, understanding the cause of the appearance of doctrines of non-violence and so-called superhuman occurrences throughout time. The approximate notion of the reality of free consciousness, living in a *momentum optimum continuum*, is perhaps more important than the exact understanding of energy and the black hole.

Doubtless, visions equal to this one have, throughout the millenniums, launched the foundations upon which all religious beliefs were built. This living vision allowed me to arrive at various conclusions. In the future, all intelligent beings will live without form or the influence of time, in a mental world.

As such, there will be no sex, the most popular human sport. Why would there be, if we would all live in a permanent orgasmic state? We would not have food, as there would neither be stomachs nor hunger. We would not have arms or legs, as the consciousness could manifest itself where it wished. We would be free from our slavery to the soma, the organism which we spend the major part of human life taking care of. We would live without the necessity for sleep, remain in a continuous state of euphoria, and have an awareness beyond the construct of days and nights.

This will be the existence that we will all live, without exception, with our thoughts alone, confronting the consequences of our acts openly in a process incapable of being escaped from, hidden or disguised. It will be a total life, without simulations, conventionalism or hypocrisy. We will all be free from appearances, labels or any other hallmark of matter.

Later on, we will also free ourselves from the psychosoma and exist without the influence of time, in a present-based process, in a condition that humankind is decidedly incapable of understanding, even as utopia. This will only be achieved through projection.

Without using any measurements of distance, weight, or known evaluation of the human problem, the reality of free consciousness is more authentic and unforgettable than all else held to be real in an entire life.

Illnesses, physical indispositions, weaknesses, deficiencies, egotism and selfishness were minimized to microscopic proportions by another all-encompassing truth. There is no need for, or value in, radicalism, irreconcilability, orthodoxy or excess.

Why do we live with conflict, shock, absurdities, vanity and stubbornness in this ephemeral human life? It is better to be liberal, optimistic, active in community efforts, independent in the face of public disagreement, open-minded towards change, and coherent and mature in our actions.

How can we reconcile this burning and constant reality with life's trivialities and tribulations? How can we live with the daily habits and the demands of the body? The power of reflection increases in importance and everything is derived from thought. The biggest pains, trials and ordeals of human existence being so insignificant, disappear as ridiculous and infantile before this enduring peace and happiness. Everything is under omnipresent and omniscient control.

Down with tears, up with smiles! The poetry of pain has fallen. *There is good humor even in multidimensionality.* There will be an ideological renewal, as well as a deepening of universalistic, evolutionary ideas. It is of prime importance to prepare for cosmic life, in conviviality with the universe, renouncing planetary sectarianism. Religious misunderstandings lose their justification at any level. One no longer believes, one knows. Transcending belief and faith, one possesses knowledge in the path towards continuous consciousness.

PROJECTIVE QUESTIONNAIRE

As an apprentice and fact finder, it is always useful to hear about the experiments of others. Thousands of these lucid occurrences take place and their authors do not make them public for various reasons. Hoping that this volume will be of practical value by encouraging readers to communicate their experiences, I present here a questionnaire for the projector. Please give frank answers to the questions that you consider pertinent. I invite you to send in your responses to this questionnaire for entry into our research databank.

1. Where, when and how do you project?

2. What is the best method for projecting yourself?

3. Describe your first lucid projection.

4. How do you distinguish between daydreams, dreams and visions?

5. What is the difference between extraphysical somnambulism and projection?

6. What are the differences between morphothosenes and real extraphysical images?

7. Do you usually dream at the beginning and end of your projections?

8. Have you ever dreamed that you were projected?

9. Do you receive help to project? Explain.

10. Have you performed technical experiments during projections? Describe.

11. Have you ever remained lucid from the beginning to the end of a projection?

12. Have you ever had a spontaneous projection?

13. Have you ever had consecutive projections?

14. Have you ever had recurrent projections?

15. Have you ever had an exceptional experience outside of the soma related to time? Describe.

16. Have you ever had projections related to the past? Explain.

17. Have you ever had projections related to the future? Explain.

18. Have you ever had experiences with children outside of the soma? Describe.

19. Have you ever had an exceptional experience with morphothosenes?

20. Do you notice any communication factor in projections? What?

21. Have you ever experienced the vibrational state?

22. Describe your most prolonged projection.

23. Describe your most noteworthy projection.

24. Describe your most exceptional takeoff.

25. Describe your most exceptional landing.

26. Describe the most picturesque extraphysical event you have experienced.

27. Describe the best extraphysical district you have experienced.

28. Have you ever observed your soma while projected?

29. Have you ever seen the interior of your soma while outside of it? Describe.

30. Have you ever touched your soma while outside of it? Where? Describe any effects.

31. Have you ever seen your soma while the psychosoma was inside?

32. While projected, do you see yourself nude or clothed? Always?

33. Has your extraphysical form ever appeared luminescent?

34. Have you ever noticed any difference in your weight outside of the soma?

35. How do you perceive the nature of the psychosoma?

36. Have you ever observed a center of power in the extraphysical form?

37. Have you ever looked at yourself in a mirror while projected? What did you see?

38. Have you ever seen yourself partially projected? Describe.

39. Have you ever seen your shadow while in the sun, while outside of the soma?

40. Have you ever suffered any physical repercussions while projected?

41. Have you ever felt projective catalepsy?

42. Have you ever passed through human beings while traveling outside the soma?

43. Have you ever communicated through a human medium (channeler)? Describe.

44. Have you ever heard sounds upon leaving or entering the soma?

45. What is your normal cardiac frequency?

46. Do you have any chronic illnesses? Which ones?

47. Have you ever experienced iperfect takeoffs and/or imperfect landings? Describe.

48. What influences you most during projections? Explain.

49. Does breathing influence projections? How?

50. Does the weight of the soma interfere with projection? How?

51. Are chewing muscles related to the process of projection? How?

52. Are cranial muscles active during projection?

53. Have you ever moved physical objects while projected? Which ones?

54. Does the silver cord exist? Explain.

55. What is the physical location of the silver cord?

56. Does the stump of the silver cord remain on the psychosoma after biological death?

57. How do you imagine the condition of the silver cord during psychic surgery, laparotomy or thoracotomy?

58. Do you find twists or knots in the silver cord? Describe.

59. Have you ever experienced double consciousness (simultaneous lucidity in the intraphysical and extraphysical dimension)?

60. Have you ever projected yourself more than once in a day? Describe.

61. Have you ever had a sudden, unintentional projection? Describe.

62. Have you ever projected while the biological soma was standing? Describe.

63. Have you ever projected while inside a moving vehicle? Describe.

64. Have you ever projected while your soma was moving? Describe.

65. Have you ever projected while your physical eyelids were open? Describe.

66. Have you ever projected during a storm? Describe.

67. Have you ever strolled through an extraphysical city? Describe.

68. Have you ever projected to another planet? Describe.

69. Have you ever visited a formless extraphysical environment? Describe.

70. Have you ever seen yourself while projected in the mentalsoma? Describe.

71. How good is your recollection of projection-related events?

72. Have you ever exercised psychic capacities while outside the soma? How?

73. Have you ever encountered force fields outside of the soma? Describe.

74. What do you have to say about flying?

75. Have you ever met someone who has recently begun their period between intraphysical lives?

76. Have you ever met a lucid projected friend?

77. Do you know a pregnant woman who projected?

78. Do you know projectors who have any missing or severely mutilated major appendages?

79. Do you know any projectors who are blind from birth?

80. Have you ever seen animals while outside of the dense body? Describe.

81. Have you ever seen an exotic extraphysical artifact? Describe.

82. Have you ever experienced surprises while outside the human body? Describe.

83. Describe your strongest emotion during a projection.

84. Has anyone ever identified you as an extraphysical consciousness while you were outside the soma? Explain.

85. Did you ever learn any lessons while in the extraphysical dimension? Explain.

86. Is there a physical constitution best suited for projection? If so, what?

87. Are there hereditary factors that predispose one to have projections? If so, which ones?

88. Do infancy and/or advanced age predispose one to having projections?

89. Can projection cure illnesses? Explain.

90. How do you regard sexuality outside of the human body?

91. Have you ever had an experience that could be interpreted as sexual while outside the physical body?

92. What factors, if any, are prejudicial to projection?

93. What is the greatest obstacle to projection? Why?

94. Have you ever had any confrontations with extraphysical consciousnesses? What happened?

95. Are there any dangers in projection? Explain.
96. Are there human beings who cannot consciously project themselves? Why?
97. Do you keep a diary of projections?
98. Does unethical conduct interfere with the processes of projection? Why?
99. Do you foresee a value in projection in the future? Why?
100. How do you perceive a world of inhabitants with continuous lucidity?

Waldo Vieira
C.P. 70,000 - CEP 22422-970
Rio de Janeiro, RJ
Brazil
phone/fax: (021) 221.8954

January 1, 1980.

GLOSSARY

The following are denominations, expressions and their equivalents that are frequently and freely used interchangeably throughout the text of this book.

Aligned state – Superimposition of the bodies of the holosoma (see glossary). Depending on the manifestation, the bodies can be aligned, in non-alignment, entering into alignment, etc.

Balloonment – Sensation of swelling or inflating like a balloon.

Clarification task – Advanced personal or group task of enlightenment or clarification.

Cleansing projection – Assistential projection that treats imbalanced extraphysical consciousnesses and removes their influence from oneself or others.

Consciential – Of or pertaining to the consciousness.

Consciential energy – Immanent energy when used, and thereby formatted, by the consciousness; animic energy; animic force.

Conscientiology – the science that studies the consciousness in an integral, multidimensional manner.

Consciousness, the – Intelligent component; soul; spirit; spiritual component; the intelligent component which animates the mentalsoma which, in turn, animates the psychosoma which, finally, animates the soma in accordance with biological laws.

Consolation task – An elementary-level personal or group *assistential task of consolation.*

Continuous lucidity – The event of the consciousness remaining alert during the entire process of a projection; the state of a person or extraphysical consciousness that remains continuously lucid; continuous wakefulness; uninterrupted lucidity; uninterrupted wakefulness.

Cosmoethic – Universal, extraphysical rules above the principles of social morality, euphemisms, formalities, and human laws and labels.

Crustal dimension – Coexisting extraphysical duplicate of the intraphysical dimension.

Dream image – Image which occurs during dreams; oniric images.

Existential series – Serial intraphysical lives; rebirth cycle; successive intraphysical existences or lives; physical rebirths in series; human or intraphysical life. Synonym outdated through overuse: reincarnation.

Exteriorization of energy – Emission, transmission, or donation of energy; the willful act by the consciousness of sending energy outwards from itself through one or more of its vehicles.

Extraphysical – Relating to that which is outside or apart from the dense intraphysical state or, in other words, less physical than the soma and ordinary physical shapes and forms; that which exists in hyper-space; that which is 4-dimensional.

Extraphysical bait – A person in the waking state to whom sick, semi-conscious extraphysical consciousnesses have become attached spontaneously or through the intervention of helpers for the purpose of being treated.

Extraphysical consciousness – The consciousness when finally free of the soma. State of the consciousness after the soma is deactivated.

Extraphysical dimension – Non-physical dimension or plane.

Extraphysical sphere of energy – An area of dense energy extending approximately 13 feet in all directions from the head of the individual.

Final projection – Last projection; definitive integral projection; permanent projection; deactivation of the soma; biological death.

First death – Biological death; the discarding of the soma.

Free consciousness – A consciousness that has transcended the rebirth cycle.

Golden cord – Subtle energetic connection between the psychosoma and mentalsoma.

Helper – A beneficent extraphysical consciousness who aids the projector to project and while projected; multidimensional companion; invisible auxiliary; intangible mentor; spirit guide; guardian angel.

Holo-chakra – Totality of all chakras; energetic system; etheric double; etheric body; energetic double; energetic body; pranic body.

Holosoma – The soma, holo-chakra, psychosoma and mentalsoma, when considered as a whole.

Hours of human anguish – From 6:00 to 10:00 p.m.

Immanent energy – Primary energy, totally impersonal, neutral and dispersed in all objects or physical creations throughout the universe; *chi* (China); *prana* (India).

In-block recollection – Remembrance of a projection in its entirety after returning to the soma.

Integral memory – Extraphysical memory; complete data bank of all things, events, sensations, etc. that the consciousness has experienced in any dimension since its inception.

Intermissive course – Sum total of disciplines and theoretical and practical experiences administered to an *extraphysical consciousness* during its period of *consciential intermission* between two *intraphysical* lives. This course occurs when one has achieved a determinate evolutionary level in one's cycle of personal existences. It has the aim of allowing *consciential completism* in the next *intraphysical life.*

Intermissive period – The *extraphysical* period between 2 of a *consciousness' existential seriations* or intraphysical lives (*rebirth cycle*).

Intraphysical dimension – physical dimension.

Intruder – An imbalanced extraphysical consciousness who tries to hinder a person through harassment and/or manipulation.

Landing – Act of the psychosoma and/or mentalsoma reentering the biological body; recoincidence; reintegration; return of the consciousness to the organic form during projection.

Mentalsoma – Vehicle of the consciousness utilized when manifesting independent of the physical body, energetic body, and psychosoma; mental body; soma of discernment; intellectual body.

Mnemonic – Pertaining to the memory.

Morphothosene – Thosene having form (and therefore necessarily denser); thought-form; extraphysical creation; ideoplastic form; mental model; mental form shaped or modeled and organized by the energy dynamics of thoughts, as directed by the will and enriched by the imagination of the intraphysical or extraphysical consciousness.

Non-alignment – The non-alignment of the bodies of the holosoma; departure of the consciousness from the soma; projection.

Physical – Relating to that which is in a dense intraphysical state: that which is 3-dimensional.

Physical base – Locale from which the consciousness projects itself (e.g., soma, bedroom, etc.).

Intraphysical consciousness – Physical consciousness; the consciousness while manifested in the physical body; man or woman; human being.

Projectiology – Science that studies projection of the consciousness and its effects, including the emission of consciential energy from the soma.

Projection – Act of projecting the consciousness out from the physical body; animic flight; animic trip; astral projection; conscious exteriorization; departure of the consciousness from alignment of the bodies with the holosoma; non-alignment of the bodies; disconnection; disembodiment; disengagement; dislocation; dissociation; ectosomatic experience; ectosomatization; exteriorization of the astral body and/or the mental body; extraphysical disengagement; Out-of-Body Experience (OBE); preview of death; psychic excursion; sidereal departure; unfolding of the personality; *vardögr*, or the arrival phenomenon (Norway); *videha* (India); waking sleep. I would like to make it clear that some of the projections of the consciousness mentioned here are projections of the mentalsoma or the mentalsoma acting independently.

Projector – One who engages in the projection of the consciousness; one who projects the mentalsoma or psychosoma whether accidentally, spontaneously, intentionally or by provocation (self-induced projection); projection operator; *dovidja* (India: twice-born); practitioner of projection; projectionist; psychic.

Projectarium – The physical space tailored so as to maximize projectability.

Psychophonic monologue – Information delivered by an extraphysical consciousness through the vocal apparatus of the soma of a projected individual.

Psychosoma – bioplasmatic soma (Russia); double; emotional body; energy-body; plastic mediator; psychic body; second body (Parapsychology); astral body.

Psychotic post-mortem – Extraphysical consciousness in a disoriented, imbalanced state.

Second death – The discarding of the remaining energies of the holo-chakra from the psychosoma.

Self-energization – Emission of consciential energy from the psychosoma of a consciousness to its own soma.

Self-induced projection – Disengagement of the mental-soma or psychosoma provoked by the will of the projector.

Silver cord – Energetic bond which keeps the psychosoma attached to the soma; cord of light; current of radiant energy; energetic communication; energetic cord; phosphorescent tail; vital bond; vital electromagnetic bond.

Soma – human body; physical body; bones, muscles and organs of a man, woman or child; densest vehicle of manifestation of the consciousness.

Supine position – Position of lying down on one's back; dorsal position.

Takeoff – Disengagement of the consciousness wherein the psychosoma and/or the mental soma temporarily leaves the soma. It sometimes indicates the isolated manifestation of the mental-soma.

Third death – Discarding of the psychosoma. This death marks the completion of the rebirth cycle.

Thosene (**tho**ught + **sen**timent + **e**nergy) – Unit of practical manifestation of the consciousness, according to conscientiology, which considers thought or concept, sentiment or emotion, and consciential energy to exist together inextricably.

Vehicles of manifestation of the consciousness – Tools or bodies in which the consciousness manifests itself in the intraphysical and extraphysical dimensions; soma, psychosoma, and mental-soma (the energetic soma does not transport the consciousness).

Vibrational state (VS) – Condition of maximum mobilization of the energies of the holo-chakra through the impulse of the will. Frequently precedes the conscious takeoff of the psychosoma.

Visual projection – Generation of morphothosenes (thought-forms) during a projection; ideoplastic projection.

ALPHABETICAL INDEX BY SUBJECT

This index allows discrimination of subjects for the purpose of providing a general scope as well as for the detailed analysis of the described projections. The Introduction and the Glossary were not included.

**IIPC - INTERNATIONAL INSTITUTE OF
PROJECTIOLOGY AND CONSCIENTIOLOGY**

The International Institute of Projectiology and Conscientiology (IIPC) is a non-profit institution of research and education, or laboratory-school, that has been dedicated to the study of the consciousness and its bioenergetic and projective manifestations (out-of-body experiences) since its foundation in 1988.

Having the objective of disseminating its *conscientiology* and *projectiology* research findings to researchers and the public, IIPC has published various books and has developed a regular program of educational activities, conferences, courses, lectures, workshops and other activities at all of its offices. Groups of foreigners regularly visit the Institute, which is able to give its courses in Portuguese, English, Spanish and French.

IIPC Statistics (1997)

Offices:
• 68 offices including:
>   1 main office in Rio de Janeiro
>   1 Center of Higher Studies of the Consciousness: in Iguassu Falls
>   9 National offices: Belo Horizonte, Brasília, Curitiba, Florianópolis, Foz do Iguaçu, Porto Alegre, Rio de Janeiro, Salvador and São Paulo.
>   7 international offices: *Barcelona, Buenos Aires, Lisbon, London, Miami, New York, Ottawa.*

• 53 research groups, divided into 7 areas:

Consciousness Research Group	*Number of groups in IIPC*	*Number of researchers*
Cutting-edge Research Group	*16*	*67*
Conscientiological Intraphysical Society	*05*	*28*
Conscientiotherapy	*04*	*24*
Group of Existential Recyclers	*13*	*91*
Group of Existential Invertors	*15*	*96*
Computer Science Group	*04*	*19*
Independent Research	*-----*	*46*
TOTAL	*57 Groups*	*371 Researchers*

Group and individual research activities began in 1992. All researchers are IIPC collaborators.

Mailing List. 87,085 individuals & institutions including: national mailing list totaling 83,163 (27,289 students) and an international mailing list totaling 3,771 (in 74 countries).

Educational Activities. IIPC has developed two types of courses:

Regular Courses include those with and without prerequisite. The five stages (in English) with prerequisite provide information on the history, ideas and research results achieved over the last 30 years in the field of conscientiology and projectiology, as well as teaching and allowing practice with various advanced techniques. Non-prerequisite courses are held along with those having pre-requisites and help in the development of students and researchers.

Extracurricular Courses - also without prerequisite, these courses are a result of the research performed by IIPC teachers in the specializations of conscientiology, projectiology and diverse fields of study in conventional science, with a consciential approach. Human sexuality, existential inversion and penta (personal energetic task) are among the themes addressed.

Lectures - As well as the courses developed by IIPC, free public lectures are held regularly at all IIPC offices.

IIPC INTERNATIONAL OFFICES

South America
Since 1992, the *Buenos Aires*, Argentina office has operated as a base serving to integrate conscientiology and projectiology in South American countries, as well as the rest of Latin America. It is connected with the implantation of the *Caracas*, Venezuela office at the other extreme of the continent.

North America
The *New York* and *Miami* offices have been giving activities in English, Spanish and Portuguese since 1994. In this way, they have been addressing the needs of Americans, Brazilian immigrants and Spanish-speaking and other interested individuals. The New York office currently offers the CDP in New York, New Jersey, Connecticut and Massachusetts.

It maintains contact with various institutions, including the American Society for Psychical Research (ASPR), one of the oldest and most important parapsychology research institutions in the world. The Miami office, established in 1994, holds its activities in both English and Spanish. The *Ottawa*, Canada office holds public lectures and offers IIPC courses on a regular basis.

Europe

In Portugal, the *Lisbon* office has been offering its activities since 1994, serving as a point of entrance for the new ideas of conscientiology and projectiology to the Old World. Together with the *London*, England (since 1995) and more recent *Barcelona*, Spain, offices, the Lisbon office maintains contact with European researchers, most notably in France and Italy, thus furthering the realization of IIPC activities and the opening of new offices in these countries.

Having the multi-dimensional and cosmo-ethical objective of catalyzing the holomaturity of more aware pre-serenissimus, IIPC is open to all researchers who are motivated to collaborate with its advanced proposals. If you are interested in working as a mini-cog of the maximechanism of conscientiality, contact the IIPC office nearest you.

IIPC Main Office: Rua Visconde de Pirajá, 572 / 6° andar

Rio de Janeiro, RJ 22410-002, Brazil

Tel.:(021) 512-9229 Fax(021) 512-4735

E-mail: *iipc@ax.apc.org*

Homepages: http://www.iipc.org.br

http://members.aol.com/iipnyusa/iipc.htm

Center for Higher Studies of the Consciousness:

C. P. 1027 - Centro - Foz do Iguaçu

PR - CEP 85851-000

Tel. / Fax (045) 525-2652

E-Mail – ceaec@foznet.com.br

Home Page – http://www.foznet.com.br/ceaec

INTERNATIONAL OFFICES

London: BMIIP London WC1N 3XX
Londres - Inglaterra
Tel.: (44181) 342.8850
E-mail: iipclonuk@aol.com

Miami: 7800 SW 57 Ave. - Suite 207 - D
South Miami, Fl 33143 - USA
Tel.: (+1305) 668.4668
Fax: (+1305) 668-4663
E-Mail: iipcflusa@aol.com

New York: 20 East, 49 Street, 2F
New York, 10017, NY - USA
Tel. / Fax (718) 721-6257
E-Mail: iipcnyusa@aol.com

Ottawa: 60 Laurie Court
Kanata, ON - K2L - 1S4, Canada
Tel. (613) 831.4483
E-Mail: iipcotwca@cybernus.ca

Barcelona: Calle Consell de Cent, 425/ 3° E
L'Example 08009 Barcelona - Espanha
Tel.: (343) 232.8008
Fax: (343) 232.8010
E-Mail: iipcbar@ibm.net

Buenos Aires: Calle Azcuenaga, 797 / 2°A - Capital Federal
CP 1029 – Buenos Aires – Argentina
Tel. / Fax: (541) 951.5048
E-Mail: iipcbsas@interactive.com.ar

Lisbon: R. Paschoal de Melo 84 - 1° Esquerdo - Sala 11
Estefania 1000 - Lisboa - Portugal
Tel. / Fax: (3511) 353.6339
E-Mail: iipclxpt@mail.telepac.pt

NATIONAL OFFICES

Belo Horizonte: R. Ulhoa Cintra, 95 / 1202
Belo Horizonte - MG - CEP 30150-230
Tel. / Fax (031) 241.1358
E-Mail – iipcbh@task.com.br

Brasília: SEPS 714/914 SUL - Ed. Porto Alegre
Bl.A - T. 28 - Asa Sul - DF - Cep 70390-145
Fone / Fax (061) 346.5573
E-Mail - iipcbsb@solar.com.br

Curitiba: R. Visconde de Nácar, 1505 / 9° Andar - Centro
Curitiba - PR - CEP 80410-201
Tel. / Fax (041) 233.5736
E-Mail – iipcctb@mps.com.br

Florianópolis: Av. Rio Branco, 354 - sala 810 - Centro
Florianópolis - SC - CEP 88015-200
Tel. (048) 224.3446 - Fax (048) 222.4002
E-Mail – iipcfln@matrix.com.br

Porto Alegre: R. Gen. Andrade Neves, 159/ cj. 12
Centro - Porto Alegre - RS- Cep 90010-210
Tel. / Fax (051) 224.0707
E-Mail - iipcpoa@pro.procergs

São Paulo: R. Augusta, 2333 - S/loja - Jd. América
São Paulo - SP - CEP 01413-000
Tel. / Fax (011) 3064.9880
E-Mail – iipcsp@ibm.net

For information on other offices, contact IIPC's main office.

CONSCIENTIOLOGICAL COMPLEX PROJECT

The *Conscientiological Complex Project* is being implanted in Iguacu Falls, Paraná, Brazil at Brazil's border with Paraguay and Argentina. This is a strategic location for the international dissemination of the ideas of conscientiology, as it is the second largest touristic center of Brazil, the third largest commercial center in the world, has a significant quantity of immanent energy, resulting from the waterfalls of Iguassu Falls, the plants, forest and geo-energy (earth energy), the reservoir of potable water from Botucatu (the largest hydroelectric dam in the world), and others.

This is a development project having an area of 24.2 acres (9.68 hectares) including its areas of environmental preservation. The objective of the Conscientiological Complex is to create a center for consciousness research.

Center for Higher Studies of the Consciousness
This universalist complex is open to consciousness researchers and exchanges with other institutions. Its aim is to benefit society through educational, scientific, technological business and ethical solutions, serving to accelerate group evolution.

The layouts of the existing buildings of the Center are adaptable to accommodate various types of uses. For example, the pavilions that have been constructed as central areas and are in the vicinity of the "Zero Coordinate" (marking the intersection of Brazil with Paraguay and Argentina) can be used for research, meetings, work with children, movies, or any other activity that arises.

Another example is the event room, which can accommodate up to 800 persons and is used for lectures, symposia, immersion courses, gathering areas and for workshops. The Extension in Conscientiology and Projectiology 2 (ECP2) course is being given on a regular basis in this room. This building will eventually accommodate research laboratories.

The following are spaces that were included in the Center's initial plans:

• The *Projectarium* is a laboratorial building that combines elements that are ideal for engendering lucid projection of the consciousness.

• The *Holo-archive* is a display facility for the permanent exposition of artifacts of knowledge that will be distributed among dozens of stands and will include space for 100,000 books that will include Dr. Waldo Vieira's library, which is composed of 52,000 volumes, being one of the most specialized in the world on subjects regarding the consciousness.

• **Immersion Courses**, like Extension in Conscientiology and Projectiology 1 (ECP1) and Extension in Conscientiology and Projectiology 2 (ECP2), that are given over weekends and require exclusive accommodations.**Conscientiotherapy (consciousness therapy) Clinic**, for public consultations.

• **Event Pavilion** – a large building in which all IIPC activities are concentrated, such as congresses, forums, symposiums, conferences workshops, assemblies, video and film screenings, etc.

• **Lodging for researchers** – a hotel service for those engaged in the activities of the Center.

• **Publishing House** and **Print Shop** for the literary productions of the Center, IIPC and others.

• **Conscientiological School**, allowing individuals to work in a manner consistent with the consciential paradigm.

- **Environmental Recuperation** of the entire area, including a wooded area comprising 20% of the total area of the Center. This will be devoted to planting fruit-bearing, medicinal and bird-attracting plants, forest recuperation and landscaping with native plant species.

- **Conscientiological Administration** – a building that would join the teams that will administrate the Center. These teams will also offer administrative assistance to interested professional companies.

The Center's pilot plan includes innovative principles that aim to increase the researchers' effectiveness, focusing on *mentalsomatics*. The *holo-archive* is the central building of this project and a holo-archive focused on youth, as well as other constructions, surround it.

The Center's construction and administration is being achieved through a cooperative system, as this presents a structure that is more resonant with the ideas of conscientiology and has a non-profit profile. For this reason, the IIPC Collaborator Cooperative was created with 209 participants in April of 1997. The administrative base of the Center is currently responsible for dissemination, marketing, contact with national and international IIPC offices, event organization and project execution.

Conscientiological Residential Complex. This complex already includes 55 condominiums and 1 model unit. The design of these homes is a rounded one, composed of three modules: bedroom/living room, kitchen and bathroom. This is a laboratory of constructive techniques that is open to visits during the Center's events. This first concrete consciential gestation is the Center's suggestion for a lifestyle that can accommodate the profile of the consciousness researcher, and represents a minimal module.

The models available for future condominiums, that can be tailored to suit the individual's needs, have space for performing **penta**, research, and to accommodate a personal library, among other factors. The residential complex will catalyze group and individual existential programs and allow the residents to work in an environment of heightened conviviality. This tends to predispose those individuals engaged in this mega-challenge to an inevitably greater self-knowledge, and an unprecedented self-confrontation within a group of persons interested in evolution of the consciousness.

Service Shopping Center. The Conscientiological Complex includes plans for a shopping center that will offer various services to the community. The Center has been offering a series of services, resources and products in its events through the *Center Express*. This concept showed itself to be very effective for the Center and has shown good results in a short period of time.

History. The events held at the Center for Higher Studies of the Consciousness have served as landmark occurrences for this research institution: 5,268 persons have already participated in the 103 activities held by the Center since December of 1996.

Research. 1997 is characterized by the implantation of research and dissemination of same. The research developed in the Center, by researchers residing both in Brazil and abroad, can be accessed through the Center's home page at: www//foznet.com.br/ceaec.

Project. The Center's work has already demonstrated that the fruits of these projects will be the result of interested individuals with an affinity for that goal living and working together.

An educational immersion is periodically realized with children at the Center that involves games, entertainment and study focusing on experiencing new techniques for allowing the attainment of effective data for the development of an adequate methodology for a conscientiological school.

Accomplishments. The Center for Higher Studies of the Consciousness produces varied dissemination material including: folders, t-shirts, buttons, caps, agendas and other items. The Center has published the following 5 books: Our Evolution, Conscientiology Editing Manual, and 3 volumes of the mini-book series. Other books that will be published include: "200 Conscientiology Theorices" and "Anthology of Multi-dimensionality".

With the support of its cooperative members and collaborators, the Center has succeeded in building 14 new and distinct constructions occupying an area of 1,129 m^2.

Magazine. The Center publishes a monthly magazine that serves to disseminate its development. The magazine is already in its 20th edition and contains articles authored by Waldo Vieira. This magazine is available by subscription.

Updates. The Center's library is already operative and includes 32,000 books donated by Dr. Vieira.

NOTES